# PUB WALKS
## IN
# Middlesex & West London

THIRTY CIRCULAR WALKS
AROUND MIDDLESEX
& WEST LONDON INNS

## David Hall &
## Rosemary Hall

COUNTRYSIDE BOOKS
NEWBURY, BERKSHIRE

COUNTRYSIDE BOOKS
3 Catherine Road
Newbury, Berkshire

ISBN 1 85306 221 9

## To our parents

Designed by Mon Mohan
Cover illustration by Colin Doggett
Photographs by David Hall and maps by the authors

Produced through MRM Associates Ltd., Reading
Typeset by Paragon Typesetters, Queensferry, Clwyd
Printed in England

# Contents

Area map showing locations of the walks.

# Introduction

Middlesex was abolished as an administrative county by the local government reforms, and now survives as a postal address, a cricketing county, and a geographical entity providing some highly rewarding walks right next to the metropolitan area.

Just to recite the names of the stations on the Metropolitan Line approaching the outer fringes is almost to quote a Betjeman poem. Look out of the window and you see rolling countryside, fields with horses and quiet churches. All a few minutes away from central London. This means that nearly all the walks are readily accessible by public transport.

This book describes nearly 140 miles of walks, each about 4½ miles long on average, ranging from some set in highly urbanised surroundings, to some absolutely rural. They include a few areas formerly in Middlesex, but transferred to neighbouring counties, and forays are made into the numbered London postal districts, but all of the walks are north of the River Thames and west of the Lea. All but two of the walks are circular: the remaining two start and finish at closely neighbouring stations on the same Underground line, so it's not the end of the world. Curiously enough, the two pubs on these walks are both called The World's End.

Apart from a worthwhile pub, each walk has a special point of interest, such as a stately home, or a historic church, or else the walk itself is in an area of special scientific interest or outstanding natural beauty. Even in very built-up areas, the walks give you an opportunity to see wildlife, either from a canal towpath, or in the tranquillity of an overgrown Victorian cemetery.

Because we think that walking beside water is special, many of the walks feature stretches alongside canals, lakes, the Thames, and some of London's lesser-known rivers, such as the Brent, the Colne and the Pinn. Although many minor rivers flow in concrete channels and are inaccessible, it is heartening to see that some with natural courses are now realised to be leisure and wildlife resources, with paths being marked out and conservation measures taken by local boroughs and other bodies. Several stretches of the recently-established Dollis Valley Greenwalk are incorporated into these walks.

A word about safety, however. If you are walking with children, please remember that most of the waterways are unfenced, and can be extremely dangerous, so do take particular care – children are always drawn to water.

The pubs have been chosen to make strangers welcome. All serve real ales, and all provide food of some sort, from simple pub meals to those which are justifiably known for the excellence of their home-cooked food. However, cooks have holidays, kitchens are renovated from time to time and changes in management can change mealtimes. If you are relying on a hot meal at a particular pub, telephone in advance. This is especially important if you are walking as a group. Eating your own sandwiches in the garden when the pub is not serving food is at best tolerated rather than welcomed. Ask first before doing this, and be discreet about it. Similarly, always ask first before leaving your car in the pub car park while walking. Most of the pubs visited were enthusiastic about the idea, but like to know who has left a car outside.

It is, of course, only polite not to tramp into a pub in muddy boots. Either eat first and go walking later, or carry a spare pair of shoes.

All of the walks are covered by Ordnance Survey Landranger Sheet 176. A London A-Z shows most of the walks, and a colour edition is particularly helpful. Carrying a compass will help to keep you on the bent and narrow, particularly in woods.

For help and information received in the preparation of this book, we should like to thank many local authority, English Heritage and National Trust staff and helpers at the various parks and houses concerned, particularly those at Trent Country Park, Forty Hall Museum, Church Farm House Museum, Marble Hill House and Chiswick House; the lay reader at St. Andrews, Totteridge; Nic and Cath Sears for writing up the Heathrow bird control measures; Roger and Lauren for introducing David to the Parkland walk; many friendly local residents who gave directions along the way; and, not least, the publicans and bar staff for patiently answering all of our questions.

David Hall and Rosemary Hall
June 1993

# ① **Hampstead Ponds**
## The Freemason's Arms

The Freemason's Arms is built on the old course of the Fleet stream, and is thought to be about 300 years old. The pub has an excellent position right next to the Heath. It is now a Bass Vintage Inn, serving home-cooked food all week. Special attractions are the enormous garden and a traditional skittles alley hidden away in the basement. At lunchtime a no-smoking dining room is available, where children can also eat with their parents. Even if you smoke, it's worth abstaining during your lunch for the sake of the decor of this room. It looks like the dining room of a grand 18th century mansion, with a blue ceiling, wooden panelling, white plaster mouldings and details picked out in plum. The decor of the remaining bar areas is similar but less opulent, with the dark wooden panelling giving a cosy atmosphere. There is plenty of comfortable seating and tables.

Beers served are Charrington IPA, Bass Bitter and Fuller's London Pride. Strongbow cider and a number of lagers are on draught, and there are a number of bottled lagers and quite a good choice of wines. Food is served Monday-Saturday 12 noon-2.30 pm and 7 pm-9 pm, and Sunday 12 noon-2.30 pm. A full menu is available during the week, ranging from salads, pasties, jacket potatoes and a tasty, spicy steak and kidney pie, to a couple of hot daily specials, one of which is always vegetarian. On Sundays a good roast is provided, together with a vegetarian alternative. Desserts and coffee are also available.

Opening times in summer are from noon to 11 pm, Monday to Saturday, and on Sunday from noon to 3 pm and 7 pm to 10.30 pm. In winter the pub closes between 3 pm and 5.30 pm on weekdays. Telephone: 071 435 4498.

*How to get there:* The pub is at No. 32 Downshire Hill, off Rosslyn Hill (A502). Nearest stations: BR – Hampstead Heath (North London line); Underground – Hampstead, Belsize Park (Northern line). Buses C11, C12, 168, 46 and 24 stop nearby.

*Parking:* No pub car park, but Hampstead Heath's large free car park is opposite, just off East Heath Road.

*Length of the walk:* 3¼ miles.

*The walk begins with a visit to Keats House before going onto the Heath. Of all London's green spaces, Hampstead Heath has the most diverse terrain and the most abundant and varied wildlife. Its woods contain over 40 species of trees. Water is an integral part of the Heath. Several streams (the most famous being the Fleet) rise on or near it, all of them eventually flowing into the Thames. This walk passes nine of the 18 ponds and each one has its own distinct character.*

**The Walk**

Leave the pub, turn right and walk up Downshire Hill, a delightful conglomeration of architectural styles from 1815, including late Regency, mock Tudor, Victorian and Gothic. Cross over the road and turn sharp left at St John's Chapel onto Keats Grove.

Cross over and continue down Keats Grove to Keats House (originally Wentworth Place), built in 1816 by Keats's friend, Charles Brown.

Leave the house, turn right and continue down Keats Grove. At South End Road, cross straight over and take the short wide path straight ahead. At the T junction turn left and walk along the curving avenue of trees to find the heath car park ahead. Follow the main path around to the right, skirting the pond. Keep on the main path which veers left, ignore the first turning right, which leads between the first and second ponds and continue along the main path which veers right to go between the second and third ponds. After the ponds, continue along the main path which now veers right and then take the right fork – with the 'no cycling' sign – and follow the path upwards to reach

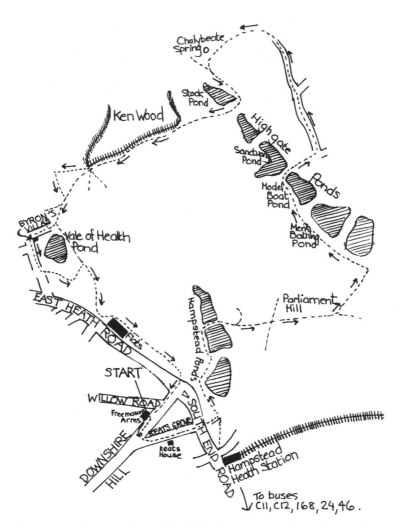

Parliament Hill, one of London's highest points (319 ft). At the top of the hill on the right is a plan to help locate some famous landmarks of the metropolis.

Continuing straight ahead, the path now goes downhill. At the next crossroads, veer left and at the T junction at the bottom of the hill turn left. Walking along this path, you will see the first of the Highgate ponds on your right. Continuing along this tarmac path you reach the second pond, the men's bathing pond. At the fork go right and continue straight ahead on the main path to the third pond (the Model Boat pond), and then the fenced-off Sanctuary Pond ahead of you.

Facing the Sanctuary Pond, turn right, go along the path and take the first right fork. At the end of this path take the third turning left into Fitzroy Park/Millfield Lane. Walk along here and, where the main road veers right, continue straight ahead. At the end of this road, go through the iron gate onto the narrow pathway ahead then almost immediately turn left and proceed down the sloping narrow path. Take the not very clearly defined narrow path veering right across the undulating meadow, keeping the two lonesome trees in the middle of the meadow to your right. Continue downhill to the tarmac path. Just before this path, to the right is the Chalybeate spring.

At the tarmac path, turn left and continue straight ahead, passing on the right the small enclosed Stock Pond. At its far end, turn right and continue straight ahead. Cross straight over the intersecting path and soon you will see a fence to the right, which borders Ken Wood. Continue along this path, ignoring all others off to the left. Eventually you come to seven diverging paths. Take the third pathway counting anticlockwise, the one to the left of a wooden railing. Walk straight ahead through the trees and the first gentle undulation, and at the next, steeper, undulation, look out for a path to the left in the middle of the dip. Take this path leading through dense trees with wooden fencing on the right. At the fork keep right and at the T junction turn right: there are toilets on the right here. About 30 yards along, take the path forking left, passing a circular brick building on the left. Just beyond this, take the path off to the left and continue downhill. Take the road which leads straight ahead, opposite the end of the path. On the left at the beginning of this road are the remains of a pub sign.

You are now entering The Vale of Health, a fascinating maze of narrow roads and alleyways of 18th and 19th century cottages. Continue along this road; the cottages on the left are Byron's Villas. Note on the left at No. 1, the blue 'D. H. Lawrence' plaque. At the top of this road turn left and a little way along look for the 'Tagore' plaque at No. 3 Villas on the Heath, just off to the right.

Continue straight ahead and turn left onto the pathway just past the end of the row of houses. Proceed along this narrow path, keeping the pond to your left and at the T junction turn left then turn right to join the main pathway which has street lights. Go straight along here passing a children's enclosure on the left.

The main path veers left, just before it reaches East Heath Road. Follow this path as it goes behind the two blocks of flats, keep going straight ahead over the open grassland. Keep on this same path and as you approach the car park you will see a wooden footbridge ahead, to the right is a stone water trough. Cross over the footbridge and enter the car park. To reach the pub turn right at the end of the car park, and cross over South End Road and Willow Road.

# Hampstead and Kenwood
## The Spaniards Inn

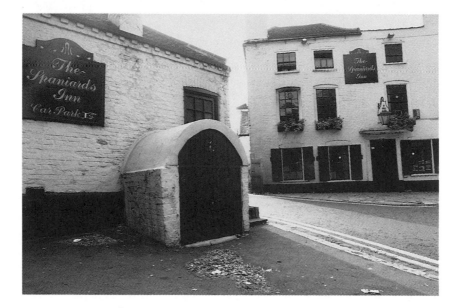

This characterful inn on the borders of Hampstead and Finchley has an outstanding history, even for the pubs of NW3. The Spanish Ambassador to James I lived in a house on the site, and many other Spaniards lived in the area, hence the name of the inn and the road on which it stands. The present pub dates from the early 18th century, and achieved fame in 1780, when the Gordon Rioters stopped for refreshment on their way to burn down Kenwood House, Lord Mansfield's country home. The landlord was an ex-butler of Lord Mansfield, and kept the mob happy with free drinks while he alerted the military. In the 19th century many famous artists and writers drank here, including Dickens, Joshua Reynolds, Leigh Hunt, Shelley, Byron, Charles Lamb and Keats. The tea party in *The Pickwick Papers* is set here, and Keats supposedly was inspired by listening to birdsong one evening in the garden to write *Ode to a Nightingale*. At least, that was what he said when his friends found him lying on his back under a tree.

Dick Turpin was the pub's most notorious customer. An upstairs oak-panelled room where he reputedly sat, selecting his next victim from the carriages passing outside, is now the Dick Turpin Cocktail

Bar. The pub has many historic prints on the walls depicting the exploits of the highwayman and scenes of the Heath, and there is also a modern Turpin family tree. The downstairs bar has an open fireplace and cosy alcoves and settles. Outside there is an attractive garden area, with both wooden and white wrought iron furniture, an arbour of wisteria and clematis, and a budgerigar aviary, set amidst a lawn bedecked with roses in summer.

Reasonably priced hot and cold bar food is available in an atmospheric room just off the main bar. At least two hot vegetarian dishes are always included and two home-made puddings (the bread and butter pudding being especially good), as well as cake and cheesecake, complete the menu. Hot food is served from 12 noon-2.15 pm, cold food until 3 pm, and in the evenings from 7 pm-9 pm (Saturday until 10 pm). Bar opening times are Monday-Saturday 11 am-11 pm and standard Sunday hours. Beers served include Young's Special, Bass, Charrington IPA, Highgate Mild, Stones, and Fuller's London Pride.

Telephone: 081 455 3276.

*How to get there:* The pub is on Spaniards Road which turns off North End Way (A502) at the Vale of Health. The pub is where Spaniards Road becomes Hampstead Lane. Nearest underground stations: Hampstead, Golders Green (Northern line). Bus 210 from Golders Green passes the pub.

*Parking:* The pub car park, or in the public car park at Kenwood House nearby.

*Length of the walk:* 4 miles (inn GR 266872).

*This easy walk combines the tranquillity of the Golders Hill Garden, and the varied flora and fauna of Hampstead Heath with the alleyways, steps and footpaths of picturesque Hampstead village. Hampstead, where imposing mansions are set among former working class cottages that are now among the most desirable and expensive in London, has long attracted prominent residents; try and keep count of the blue, brown or black plaques. We made it fourteen, but there may be more. The walk passes three former mansions open to the public, Fenton House, Burgh House and Kenwood House. Hampstead is on a hill, and throughout the walk, unexpected vistas of London are revealed. The Heath and the village are rewarding in all seasons.*

## The Walk

Turn right leaving The Spaniards Inn, taking great care as you pass between the pub and the preserved toll house opposite as the road is narrow and there is no footpath. At the first turning on the right

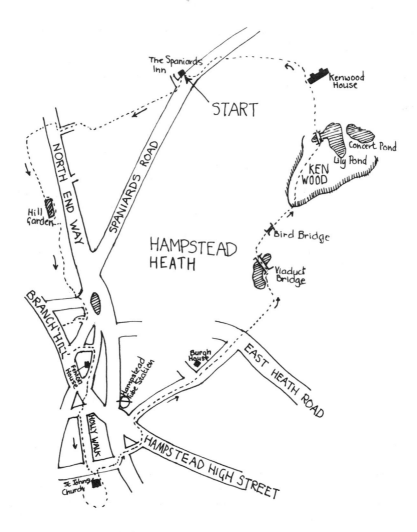

(marked 'Access to Spaniards End'), turn half right along the gravel
path barred to vehicles by a metal gate and tree stumps. Keep on this
path, which eventually comes out at North End. Go straight ahead to
the T junction, turn right onto North End Way, cross it at the zebra
crossing and continue to the entrance to Golders Hill Park. Enter the

14

park, cross the car park and take the path straight ahead cutting across the grass and through the trees. At the end, turn left, and go through the wooden gate and up the steps.

Follow the path straight ahead, and at the conifer tree take the right fork. At the end there is a fence, and the entrance gate to the Hill Gardens, a secluded park open daily from 9 am to 7.30 pm (no dogs). Enter the park, turn right, first left, and left again, and descend the steps to the pond. At its far side, climb the steps to the pergola and go halfway along this and through the wrought iron gate on the right. Take the path to the right sweeping downhill away from the pergola. Where five paths diverge, take the left downward path and turn left at the main path. Keep on this main path with the ruined, now inaccessible, part of the pergola on your left. The peaceful pond and this silent ruin give the Hill Gardens an air of romance and mystery. When the path narrows and becomes sandy, take the broader right fork uphill. At the main path, turn left, then at the top of this path turn right just before the flagpole, and take the path to the left between the grass enclosures.

Ahead is Whitestone Pond, named after an old white milestone nearby. Cross straight over West Heath Road and walk along Lower Terrace. This is the highest point in Central London, which is why, on the left, there is a radio mast, the Hampstead Astronomical and Meteorological Station, and a water reservoir. Take the first turning right onto Judges Walk. Ahead soon appears the attractive 18th century house Capo de Monti where an 'S' over the door marks Sarah Siddons's stay in 1804. Just before the house turn right through the gap in the metal railing onto the grass and left into the avenue of lime trees. At the end descend the steps, cross the road (take care), turn left, walk down Branch Hill and take the first left, back onto Lower Terrace. No. 2, on the left, has a black plaque marking Constable's stay there, when he produced many paintings of the Heath.

Now turn right into Admirals Walk. Admiral's House on the left, named after its 18th century owner, the eccentric Admiral Barton, was turned by him into a ship-like structure from which he is reputed to have fired a cannon to mark naval anniversaries. Continue along Admirals Walk, then at the crossroads turn right onto Hampstead Grove. On the right is Hampstead's oldest mansion, Fenton House (built 1695), now National Trust and open Saturday-Wednesday 11 am-6 pm April-October (Saturdays and Sundays 2 pm-6 pm during March). Admission charge (free to NT members). The house contains a collection of keyboard instruments, and the attic windows give good views over London. Admission to the beautiful typical 17th century garden is free.

Further on is the overspill churchyard to St John's, Hampstead's parish church, with its entrance at the bottom of Holly Walk. In the south east corner are memorials to a number of prominent Hampstead residents, including Hugh Gaitskell, Kay Kendall, George du Maurier and Anton Walbrook. St John's church is on the opposite side of the road and the most notable tomb there is that of Constable. To reach it take the path nearest the church saying 'no dogs' and follow it round the churchyard, admiring the views of north London, and continuing left at the wall, Constable's grave is on the right. Continue along the path and leave the churchyard at the right, along Church Row.

Turn left onto Heath Street, crossing at the zebra crossing. Take the first right onto Oriel Place, then cross over the zebra crossing onto Hampstead High Street and enter Flask Walk (named when this was a spa site). Cross New End Square onto Well Walk. On the left is Burgh House, built in 1703, open 12 noon-5 pm Wednesday to Sunday, admission free. The house has a local history collection, and regular art exhibitions in the gallery. The basement buttery has good value food (open 11 am to 5.30 pm Wednesday to Sunday).

Continue along Well Walk to the T junction and cross over East Heath Road onto Hampstead Heath. Take the path straight ahead, which soon widens to become Lime Avenue, one of the Heath's most notable paths. At the crossroads take the second left (wider) path leading up to Viaduct Pond, then follow the pond to the right to Viaduct Bridge and cross it. After about 20 yards take the first narrow path to the right. Cross the bridge ahead, nicknamed Bird Bridge by local bird watchers, and pausing there, you should see blue tits, great tits and visitors to the shrubbery such as nuthatches, wrens, tree creepers, jays and longtail tits. Beyond the bridge, keep straight ahead, passing a grove of fine old beech trees on the right.

Kenwood entrance is at the top (opening times on information board). Enter the wood, a relic of the old Forest of Middlesex, where beech and oak predominate. Keep straight ahead, fork left, turn left at the T junction then cross the bridge and go up the grassy slope to Kenwood House. The ponds on the right, home to numerous waterbirds, are Lily Pond and Concert Pond, where open air concerts are held in summer. Kenwood House, open daily, was built in the early 18th century, and passed to the Earl of Mansfield, then Lord Chief Justice, in 1754. Walk through the ivy-covered archway to the left of the house, turn left at the sign for West Gate Lodge, take the path to the car park, go through the exit onto Hampstead Lane, turn left and return to the pub.

# 3 Hampton Court
## The King's Arms

This is a wonderful old free house with a cosy congenial atmosphere, and traditional decor of dark wood panelling, antique furniture, including a few settles, wooden beams, brass plates and even sawdust on the floor of the public bar, which has an open fireplace, bar billiards, darts and a pinball machine. Board games and newspapers are available in the lounge bar. Dogs are welcome, and a drinking bowl outside proclaims 'Free dog biscuits at the bar'. The pub does a range of excellent good value hot and cold bar food, including some tempting desserts (such as gateaux and lemon meringue). The King's Arms also features a separate restaurant.

The beers served are Tanglefoot, Badger Best Bitter, Everards Old Original, Eagle Bitter, Shepherd Neame Bishops Finger and Wadworth 6X and there is an extensive wine list as well.

Food is served while the pub is open, which is 11 am to 11 pm daily, except Sundays (closed between 3 pm and 7 pm). The pub is also open for coffee from 9 am. Telephone: 081 977 1729.

*How to get there:* The pub is right next to the Lion Gate entrance into Hampton Court on Hampton Court Road (A308). Nearest stations: Hampton Court (BR) and the walk passes close to Hampton Wick (BR).

17

*Parking:* The pub has no car park, but there are several nearby, the nearest being in Hampton Court itself (car parking £1.60 at time of writing) and in Bushy Park, just past the Diana fountain (free).

*Length of the walk:* 3 miles, not including the maze.

*Hampton Court Palace is the largest and most impressive of the riverside royal palaces. This easy walk (which can be made much more difficult by tackling the maze) first passes through the delightful formal gardens of the palace grounds and then, in complete contrast, through the uncrowded Hampton Court Park, a great expanse of open countryside criss-crossed with imposing avenues of lime trees, home not only to the deer, but also to numerous water birds, which frequent secluded ponds and waterways.*

## The Walk

Walk through Lion Gate (next to the pub), the north entrance to Hampton Court Palace grounds. Then, either turn right if you want to extend the walk by completing the maze, or take the first left and follow the Laburnum Walk, continuing along the main path to a crossroads. Turn left, then go through the gate on the left onto Broad Walk, and turn right towards the palace. A little way along on the right is the Tudor Tennis Court where real (ie royal) tennis is still played on the court built for James I. Admission to the spectators' gallery is free.

Take the path leading away from the palace opposite the tennis court entrance. On your left are the formal gardens laid out for Charles II, and then the path skirts a semicircular canal.

Cross the second footbridge, and enter the park through the wrought iron gate. Deer still roam the park, first enclosed for hunting by Henry VIII. Take the gravel path along the left side of the lime tree avenue, then turn left onto the tarmac path crossing it. At the row of cottages on the left, walk across the grass on the right to the secluded Oak Pond (actually surrounded by willow trees). Walk all round the pond, where you will see, if you are lucky, a heron.

Return to the tarmac path, passing down the end of the row of cottages towards Long Water. Turn right, follow Long Water to its end, and turn left over the cattle grid. Follow the path until it veers off to the right (at an intersection signposted Gardener's Cottage and Stud House). Keep straight on over the grass, following the avenue of lime trees to Hampton Wick Pond. Just before the pond, you cross another avenue offering a short cut back to the palace if you don't wish to go on to Bushy Park. Otherwise follow the pond round to the right and leave the park at Kingston Gate straight ahead.

Cross over Hampton Court Road and walk up Church Grove (on the left of Kingston Bridge House), following the wall round Bushy Park,

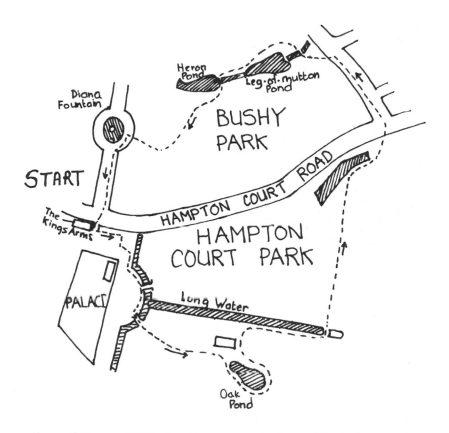

another of Henry VIII's hunting grounds, less visited, but no less attractive than Hampton Court Park. Church Grove becomes Park Road and then Sandy Lane, where Hampton Wick Gate leads into the park. Follow the tarmac path, taking the left fork. Cross over the waterway, and at the first pond leave the path and follow the embankment round the pond.

Cross the bridge just before the second pond, Heron Pond, and follow the bank round, keeping the pond on your right. Between half and threequarters of the way along the pond, take a narrow path forking off to the left behind an oak tree. The path leads through some high bracken, then you see a path to the left leading to a public convenience and on your right there is a car park. Strike out half right here, over the grass to the road in front of you. Turn left at the fountain, and follow Chestnut Avenue to leave Bushy Park by Hampton Court Gate, opposite the King's Arms where you started.

# **Bushy Park**
## The White Hart

The White Hart is a Fuller's house in this busy position near Kingston Bridge. There are several large bars cosily furnished, with much Victorian bric-a-brac, particularly old bottles and flagons. There is a separate eating area by the entrance to the lounge bar and, unusually for London pubs, there are no-smoking tables. Children can eat at these tables, and children's portions of food are available. In fine weather you can enjoy an extensive patio garden away from the bustle of the street, and there are also benches at the front. Occasional barbecues are held in the garden in summer.

A good choice of tasty food is served on weekday lunchtimes until 2 pm and on Sundays a roast lunch is served 12.30 pm-2.30 pm. Food is also normally available in the evenings six nights a week (not Sundays), depending on staff availability. The menu includes a large range of sandwiches made to order, ploughman's lunches, salads, jacket potatoes, omelettes, a variety of hot standard dishes and daily specials (such as lasagne or an imaginative bacon and sausage Kiev) – all made on the premises. Filter coffee is available. Beers served are Fuller's London Pride, Chiswick Bitter and ESB on handpump. Guinness and Strongbow are on draught, and imported bottled premium lagers are available.

The opening times are Monday and Tuesday 11 am-3 pm and 5 pm-11 pm, Wednesday-Saturday 11 am-11 pm, Sunday 12 noon-3 pm and 7 pm-10.30 pm.
Telephone: 081 979 5352.

*How to get there:* The pub is at the end (No. 70) of the High Street in Hampton Wick, next to the roundabout where it joins the A308 at Kingston Bridge. Nearest stations: Hampton Wick and Kingston (BR). Part of the walk is close to Hampton Court (BR).

*Parking:* Usually available in the pub car park, but not if the pub is catering for a function. There are car parks in Bushy Park.

*Length of the walk:* 5½ miles (inn GR 175694).

*A longer look at Bushy Park than given by Walk 3, which should give you plenty of opportunities to see the deer and birdlife which frequent it. The walk passes several ponds, and near Bushy House. The delightful Waterhouse Woodland Gardens are a highlight near the end of the walk. There are no hills or stiles to climb. The deer may be dangerous in May, June, July and October, and should not be approached too closely.*

**The Walk**
Leave the pub, turn right and then turn right again into Church Grove, passing the parish church of St. John the Baptist, a nineteenth century building designed by Edward Lapidge (who also designed St. Peter's in Hammersmith and St. Mary's in Hampton). Turn left into Park Road, followed by Sandy Lane, and then enter Bushy Park by Hampton Wick Gate.

This royal park was opened to the public in 1838. Follow the main tarmac and gravel path out half right in front of you – this is Cobbler's Walk. The park usually seems emptier of people than Hampton Court Park, and you can enjoy the silence broken only by the wind in the trees, the rooks (and the aircraft approaching Heathrow).

After crossing a small stream over a bridge, Cobbler's Walk turns to the left. Leave it and follow the grassy path straight ahead, leading to the right edge of the Warren Plantation group of trees. You may get close to deer and birds as you pass through the trees. The path then proceeds towards the Teddington Gate at the end of Chestnut Avenue.

Just after a small tree plantation on the right, you can see a white monument enclosed by railings. This marks the site of the US Army Air Force European HQ from July 1942 to December 1944. Apart from this monument, not a trace remains to mar the park. At Teddington Gate, cross Chestnut Avenue and take the path half left towards the

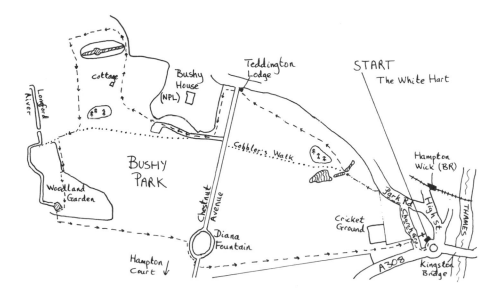

sports area. Bushy House is behind the bowling green.

Bushy House was built in the late 17th century, altered greatly in the 18th century, and was the home of the Park Ranger. Before he became king, William IV lived there with his mistress and after he died in 1837, his widow Queen Adelaide used it (although she also rented Bentley Priory, where she died). The house is now the headquarters of the National Physical Laboratory (NPL), the National Standards Laboratory, the most important aspect of whose work is metrology, the science of weights and measures, and includes establishing standards, methods of measurement and calibration tests. There is no public access to the house or gardens and the path now follows the NPL perimeter fence. Turn right onto a road crossing the path where the fence also leads off to the right.

Go past former lodge houses to Bushy House, keeping to this road which skirts the perimeter. You shortly get good views of the house and grounds on the right. Keep straight on through the car park, following the metalled road, then at the end of the car park strike out half right across the grass, aiming to clear the edge of the sports fields on the right and to the right of the fenced-in cottage (Barton's Cottage) – a path is discernible in the grass.

The path becomes better defined, following the edge of the sports field. Take the right fork at the end of the playing field, crossing a tarmac path. Come to the fence of another sports ground and follow the path towards the edge of the fenced-off plantation ahead. There is a brick wall on the right of the path, which is now a well-marked gravel path.

The plantation on the left is Canal Plantation. The canal itself can be seen behind the low brick wall, hiding beneath a covering of weeds. Ducks may be busily feeding on the surface. Just after passing the Canal Plantation, as the fence curves away to the left, take a path leading away to the half left, then turn left at an avenue of chestnut trees (not as grand as Chestnut Avenue). Follow the avenue as far as the path crossing it just before the interruption in the avenue. Turn left onto this and follow it past the end of the canal.

The path comes to a road at a small bridge. Cross the bridge, then take the second path on the right, leading away to the half right towards the round plantation ahead. Keep on the broad grassy path which passes a line of trees then veers left. After passing the right hand end of the round plantation, turn right onto the tarmac Cobbler's Walk. Turn left at the fence, and follow this path by the perimeter of the Willow Plantation.

You now come to the entrance of the Waterhouse Woodland Gardens. These are open from 9 am to dusk, but note that no dogs are allowed inside — you will have to detour around the fence if you have canine accompaniment. Enter the gardens and turn left. The fence protects the gardens from deer, and there is more shrubbery than in the open park. There is also more exotic planting and small ponds, so a more varied wildlife habitat is provided.

Stay on the gravel path straight ahead. Just before you cross a stream, keep an eye open on the right for a handsome totem pole topped by a carved bird. You then pass a little waterfall at the end of a pond with a Japanese-style pavilion. Walk up to the pavilion and look at the Waterhouse Pond on the right, with its surrounding willows and chestnuts, and the waterlilies and waterfowl. Continue on past the pavilion and turn left to follow the canal.

Leave the gardens at the gateway and turn left to follow the path and avenue towards the Diana Fountain. When you reach this, go to its right, cross the road and take the tarmac path ahead (signposted 'lavatories'). Pass to the left of the children's playground and continue to follow the path at the perimeter of Bushy Park, approaching the cricket ground. The wooded area to the right harbours squirrels and rabbits, amongst other animals.

As you approach the end of the park, keep to the right of the cricket ground, and leave the park by the metal gate, walking along the narrow chestnut avenue. This ends at the parish church in Church Grove – turn right and then left to return to the pub.

# **Trent Country Park**
## 5 The Cock

The Cock, in Chalk Lane, Cockfosters, is a 20th century brick building, with a pleasant interior which is a hotchpotch of art nouveau and country cottage decor in subdued mellow tones. It attracts a mixed age clientele and the background music is unobtrusive. In fine weather the garden is peaceful, as the pub is set back from the main road.

Beers served are Benskins Best Bitter, Ind Coope Burton Ale and Tetley Yorkshire Bitter. The pub serves lunch and dinner seven days a week, a separate restaurant sometimes being opened for meals. There is a large selection of reasonably priced dishes available, with at least one vegetarian speciality daily. Their giant Yorkshire puddings with tasty fillings were our favourite. As well as hot meals, sandwiches and ploughman's lunches are served. Children are allowed in the dining area, the bar itself being for over 21s.

Lunches are available between 12 noon-2 pm all week, and dinners 5 pm-9 pm on weekdays and 7 pm-9 pm on Saturdays and Sundays. Opening hours for the pub are Monday to Saturday 11.30 am to 2.30 pm and 5.30 pm (Saturday 7 pm) to 11 pm, and on Sundays from 12.30 pm to 2.30 pm and 7 pm to 10.30 pm.

Telephone: 081 449 7160.

*How to get there:* The Cock is on Chalk Lane, just a little north of Cockfosters Underground station, off Cockfosters Road (A111) at the junction of Chalk Lane with Games Road, separated from Cockfosters Road by a recreation ground. Nearest Underground station: Cockfosters (Piccadilly line).

*Parking:* Available in the fair-sized pub car park. Car parks are also available in Trent Country Park and at Cockfosters station.

*Length of the walk:* 4½ miles (inn GR 278967).

*The walk is entirely located within Trent Country Park, 470 acres of woodland and meadows, one of the few surviving remnants of the once extensive royal hunting forest of Enfield Chase. This is a very well planted public open space, with a nature trail, a pets corner for children and a trail for the blind. There are many clear footpaths and bridleways, and the walk goes all round the estate, giving views of the house, which is now part of Middlesex University and not accessible to the public, and many opportunities to see a variety of wildlife. There is a gentle slope, but there are no stiles to climb.*

**The Walk**

Leave the pub, walk straight ahead to Cockfosters Road, turn right here and cross the road. A little way along is the main entrance into Trent Country Park. Enter the park and walk straight ahead, taking the first fork to the left. The monument on the right states that the garden was begun in 1706 and was enlarged, altered and adorned up to the year 1740. This is impossible, as the area was still part of Enfield Chase until 1777. The reason for this is that the monument is one of three introduced here from Wrest Park by the last private owner, Sir Philip Sassoon. The park's first owner was Sir Richard Jebb, physician to George III. He named the park after the Italian Tyrol town of Trento where he had attended the Duke of Gloucester, the King's brother. During the 19th century the estate was owned by the Quaker banker David Bevan who planted the magnificent double avenue of lime trees.

Continue ahead to the cafe on the left, then take the pebbled path straight ahead, just beyond the right side of the cafe and on the left of a notice board. You will see a picnic area to the right. The path goes through Oak Wood, where there are many silver birch trees amongst the oaks. At the end of this wood, cross the plank bridge over the ditch and continue straight ahead, along the left hand edge of Rookery Field, approaching a wooded area. At the end of the field, turn right and follow the path up to the avenue ahead. Turn left here to follow the avenue. Along here you will see the entrance to the woodland nature trail on the left.

Enter the nature trail, which follows a route through deciduous woodland and a path skirting a pond. Oak and hornbeam predominate in the wood, these being the most prolific trees of Middlesex's woodland, but beech, wild cherry, silver birch, horse chestnut, hawthorn, ash, elder, rowan, sweet chestnut and sycamore also grow here. In summer look out for butterflies and woodland birds. The pond is artificial and was formed by damming a small stream called the Leeging Beech Gutter. It is used by mallard, pochard, tufted duck, Canada geese, coot, moorhen and heron. In summer, yellow water lilies can be seen on its surface. Leaflets are available from the park office describing in detail the wildlife to be seen at different times of year.

Leave the circular nature trail where you came in, turn left and take the path following the fence. Soon you will see ahead of you the mansion through the trees. The original 18th century house was built for Sir Richard Jebb by the architect Sir William Chambers, who also designed Somerset House and the Kew Gardens pagoda. The house was refaced in brick in 1926 for Sir Philip Sassoon, the last private owner, who had a golf course and an airstrip constructed in the grounds. He was such a keen aviator that when he died in 1939 his ashes were scattered over the park from an aeroplane. During the Second World War the house was used to interrogate prisoners of war, including Hitler's deputy Rudolf Hess, who presumably found this a more pleasant environment than Spandau prison.

Continue along the path which veers left and goes between two fish ponds. The area beyond this was Sir Philip Sassoon's golf course. It has now been returned to open grassland. A little further along you will see an obelisk in the distance up on the left. Make your way to this either by skirting the edge of the open grassland or walking straight across it and up the clear track between the trees. The obelisk states 'To the memory of George Grey, Earl of Harold, Son of Henry and Sophia, Duke and Duchess of Kent'. This inscription has nothing to do with Trent Park, the obelisk being another of Sassoon's introductions from Wrest Park.

Facing the obelisk turn right and walk along the path following the woodpecker signs on the wooden posts. The path goes through the Moat Wood, passing the remains of Camlet Moat, an ancient earthwork, on the left. Soon you meet a main path to the left which leads to the Hadley Road entrance to the park. Ignore the woodpecker sign to the right and continue straight ahead on the pebbled path which crosses several narrow paved pathways and leads through the picnic area (past a tap and litter point). Continuing ahead, you soon see an entrance for equestrians on the left, and a bridle path now runs parallel to the footpath.

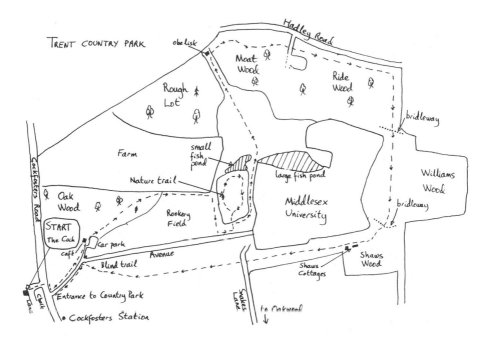

A little further on, at the edge of the park, follow the path round a 90° turn to the right, and go downhill. At the complex crossroads of bridlepaths and footpaths continue straight ahead, going through two wooden barrier gates, and go uphill. Go straight across another crossroads marked with wooden barrier gates, taking the firmer path opposite barred to vehicles and horses, but not pedestrians by the gate. This veers round to the right, skirting an open field on the right and the university buildings are beyond it.

The path becomes a metalled track at Shaws Cottages on the left. Continue straight across a broader road at the next crossroads, where there is a large signpost on the right, taking the path straight ahead running to the left of Rookery Lodge. To the left is a sports field, and tennis courts are on the right. At the end of the open field area go through a wooden barrier gate. Continue straight ahead through Church Wood, ignoring the two paths to the left. The path joins up with the Blind Trail, marked by a low tapping rail, and posts carrying information in Braille. Walk along the Blind Trail, and at the end turn left, and walk along the main driveway. Leave the park, turn right and cross over the road to reach the pub.

# 6 Forty Hall
## The King and Tinker

This may be the oldest inn in the borough of Enfield; an inn is said to have been on this site since the 12th century. Its curious name originates from a story about James I. The King, hunting in Enfield Chase, left his nobles, found an alehouse and, as an unknown stranger, shared a drink with a friendly tinker, who was later greatly surprised when he discovered his companion's identity. Copies of an old ballad telling this story, which ends with the tinker being knighted, are available at the pub, which is the alehouse where this odd couple met.

The old buildings are full of character, with many small side rooms with wooden benches, low ceilings and beams. It is a Taylor Walker house and serves Tetley Bitter, Taylor Walker Bitter, Ind Coope Burton Ale and Adnams Bitter (a guest beer) on handpump. Draught Löwenbräu and Bulmers cider, and wines and bottled lagers are available.

A wide variety of excellent pub food is served seven days a week, 12 noon – 2 pm (some items may be available in the early evenings). As well as rolls, sandwiches and ploughman's lunches, sardines, pilchards or pâté on toast, pies, and meals such as chops, chicken, gammon and scampi are served. Barbecues are often held in the summer, with roast lunches offered Sundays. Children under 14 are not allowed in the bars, but the garden is very attractive.

Opening hours are 11 am – 3 pm and 5.30 pm – 11 pm on weekdays; Sundays 12 noon – 3 pm and 7 pm – 10.30 pm.

Telephone: 081 363 6411.

*How to get there:* The pub is on Whitewebbs Lane. From Enfield, head north on the A105, called in succession Silver Street, Baker Street, Forty Hill and Bulls Cross, then turn left onto Whitewebbs Lane. The pub is just after the golf course on the left. Nearest stations: Turkey Street, Enfield Town, Gordon Hill (all BR). Buses 191 and 231 run to Forty Hall from Enfield Town.

*Parking:* In the pub car park – this stays open in the afternoon when the pub is closed.

*Length of the walk:* 4¼ miles (inn GR 331998).

*This walk takes you to Forty Hall, a Grade 1 listed 17th century building, now a museum, and through the very attractive public parkland surrounding the hall and the neighbouring Whitewebbs Park, including the gardens, wooded areas, open meadows, part of the old course of the New River and an interesting nature trail.*

**The Walk**

Leave the pub, turn right and follow the footpath on Whitewebbs Lane. Keep following the footpath as it crosses and recrosses a bridlepath along the edge of the golf course. Go across a layby and turn right, crossing a stile onto a gravel public footpath, which goes through a narrow wooded area between the golf course and farmland. The fenced path is easy to follow, and borders attractive grassland.

Cross a plank bridge over the stream, after which the path veers to the right, becomes a tarmac path and curves to the left. Cross a concrete bridge over Cuffley Brook, and at a T junction, turn left, then take the gravel path after a small plank bridge. Fork left at a junction – Cuffley Brook is on your left, and a lake begins on your right, a haven for waterfowl, with an island in the water. At the end of the lake, keep straight on, looking to your right. When you can see an avenue of trees on the right, and the house beyond this, turn right onto the narrow path and walk up the avenue towards it.

Forty Hall, built in 1629-1636 for Sir Nicholas Rainton, Lord Mayor of London 1632-33, is now a museum run by the Borough of Enfield and is open Tuesday – Sunday 10 am – 5 pm, closed Monday (admission free). As well as special temporary exhibitions, there are displays of 16th and 17th century furniture, ceramics, paintings and local history, including old maps of Middlesex.

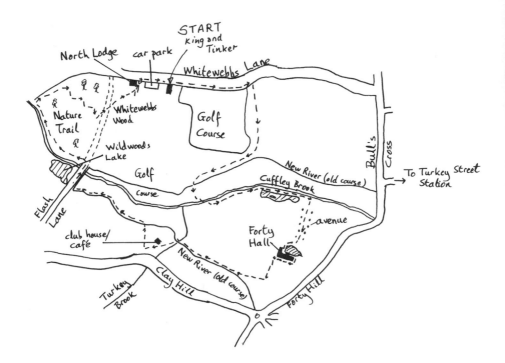

After visiting the house, go round to the back, admiring the garden, and walk along the buildings and past the cafe. Enter the walled garden. Turn left onto a fenced-off path at the edge of the field and follow it round to a gateway into a wooded area. Go straight on here, keeping the stream on your left. This area is a good spot for wrens.

Follow a gravel path over plank or log bridges, and come to a near-crossroads with a tarmac path. Turn right and cross the concrete bridge over Turkey Brook, then turn left towards the car park and golf clubhouse, following the fenced path at the edge of the golf course. There is a public cafe in the clubhouse. Walk through the car park, leaving it at the top right corner, then turn right and go downhill (on the footpath, not the more obvious bridleway to the left).

As you get to the golf course, turn left at a wooden post bearing the number 1, marking the start of a nature trail through Whitewebbs Park, public parkland since 1931.

Follow the nature trail round the edge of the field (there is no obvious path here). At post 2, follow the arrow. Continue to post 3, turn left, enter the wood, then turn right at an unnumbered post. The old course of the New River is on the left. This was constructed in

1613 by Sir Hugh Myddelton to bring drinking water from Hertfordshire to reservoirs in Islington. A loop in the New River running through this parkland was cut off in the 1850s.

Flowers typical of ancient woodland can be seen here, including celandine and dog's mercury. Cross Cuffley Brook using a brick bridge carrying an aqueduct, built in the 1820s to carry the New River over the brook, replacing a 'flash' (waterfall and pool), hence Flash Lane, the bridleway crossing the estate here. At post 4, follow the arrow to the left. Cross Flash Lane via the stiles and you can make a slight detour here by going left down Flash Lane a little way to see Wildwoods Lake. There are Chinese muntjac deer here, but rarely seen. Now return to the stiles and continue to post 5.

You can see sedges and a number of flowering plants here, and yew and holly trees. Fork right at the arrow. Wildwoods Lake is visible to the left as you walk along. Turn right at the arrow on post 6, noting the large sycamore tree. On the far bank of the stream on the left are pussy willow trees. Continue to post 7, overlooking the fields where mallow and comfrey plants can be seen by the path. As you near the road, cross the bridlepath following the white arrows, and follow the path round the edge of the wood, crossing the bridlepath again by the stile to reach post 8.

Take the left fork; an oak, hornbeam and wild service tree can be seen here. Cross the plank bridge. The wood here is a mixture of birch and beech, with small open areas and clumps of ferns. At post 9 keep straight on by the hornbeam and silver birch trees, and pass to the right of the memorial to Ranger, a horse (the inscription is, sadly, mostly worn away). Continue to follow arrows on the wooden posts, crossing Flash Lane again, then shortly after, emerge near the North Lodge entrance at a nature trail notice board. Turn left here to leave the nature trail and just after an RSPB notice board, with a giant Wellingtonia tree next to it, leave the park. Turn right at the road and walk down the road to return to the pub.

# **Harrow**
## 7 The King's Head Hotel

The pub dates from 1535 (although the façade is newer), and claims connections with Henry VIII, the king after whom it is named. Henry may have stayed here while hunting. It is a fascinating rambling old building with many bars, nooks and crannies with a Tudor interior including lots of traditional dark wood furniture, and an interesting garden at the rear giving fine rural views. As a Harrovian known for enjoying a drink, it is no surprise that Churchill is said to have been just one of its many famous patrons.

This old inn still provides accommodation (over 40 rooms are available), and one of the bars acts as the dining room. Children can eat here with their parents. The menu concentrates on hot meals, of which there is a wide range, including a large choice of very good, reasonably priced pizzas and Indian dishes are sometimes available. The restaurant is basically open during the bar hours.

The beers served are Wadworth 6X, Ruddles County and Theakston Old Peculier, with two lagers on draught. Weston's Cider is available, and there is a reasonable selection of bottled beers, imported lagers and a wine list. Opening times for the bar are: Monday – Saturday 11 am – 3 pm, 5.30 pm – 11 pm, Sunday 12 noon – 3 pm, 7 pm – 10.30 pm. Telephone: 081 422 5541.

*How to get there:* The King's Head is on The Green at the junction of High Street and Byron Hill Road in Harrow-on-the-Hill. Nearest stations: Harrow-on-the-Hill (Metropolitan line). The walk also passes next to Northwick Park (Metropolitan line) and close to Sudbury Hill (Piccadilly line and BR) and South Kenton (Bakerloo line/BR).

*Parking:* There are a few spaces in front of the pub and some on-street parking in the surrounding streets.

*Length of the walk:* 5 miles (inn GR 151870).

*Harrow-on-the-Hill is one of Middlesex's highest villages. The walk begins in the attractive village itself, which is dominated by the 19th century Gothic Revival buildings of Harrow School, and has many fine Georgian buildings on and near the High Street. From the churchyard you have imposing views of London and the surrounding counties. The walk then descends from the hill, passing along footpaths and recreation fields to return to Harrow through the school playing fields.*

**The Walk**
On leaving the pub turn left and walk along the High Street, attractively lined by Georgian buildings.

Opposite the Vaughan Library, by Sir George Gilbert Scott, and the school chapel (1854, also by Scott), turn left into Church Hill signposted Old Speech Room Gallery and St. Mary's Church. The Old Speech Room, on the left, is now the school's museum and art gallery (Harrovian artists include Victor Pasmore and of course Churchill). It is open daily, except Wednesdays, 2.30 pm – 5 pm, admission free. This building is part of the Old School complex, which contains the original schoolhouse from 1615, now called the Fourth Form Room. The school was founded in 1571 by John Lyon, a farmer, to provide free education for local boys but soon began to attract fee-paying boys from further afield. It expanded greatly in the 19th century and most of the present buildings date from this time. No less than seven British Prime Ministers were Harrovians and other famous pupils included Byron and Trollope.

A little further up the road is St. Mary's church, founded in 1087 by Archbishop Lanfranc, the lower part of the tower remaining from this time. The upper part and the spire, which can be seen for miles around, were added in 1540. The nave was rebuilt in 1235. The church was heavily restored by Sir George Gilbert Scott in 1849.

Enter the churchyard by the lychgate and, walking along the side of the church to the western end, turn left at the T junction. Up on the left protected by an iron grille is the 'Peachey Stone' (the tomb of John Peachey) where Byron used to sit and stare at the view. Byron's daughter Allegra (died age five) is buried under the church porch.

After admiring the view continue down to the right onto Roxborough Park and take the path to the right signposted Public Footpath to Harrow, which leads onto The Grove Open Space. Continue along the tarmac path to Lowlands Road and turn right, following a footpath past the war memorial and then take the first right up Grove Hill.

Take the narrow Davidson Lane to the left, Peterborough Road, turn left and walk downhill a short distance to the path on the right (next to Garlands) signposted Public Footpath to Watford Road. This is Northwick Walk. The path has a canopy of trees which attracts many birds in summer; in winter it can get extremely muddy. Walk to the end and at the main road, Watford Road, turn left and go under the subway. Turn right at the end, taking the exit signposted Hospital. Walk past the Harrow campus of the University of Westminster and take the footpath to the left between the college and the hospital. At the back of the hospital, follow the path round to the left, and, just before the entrance to Northwick Park Underground, turn right onto the tarmac Proyers Path, a route marked by lampposts.

After a dog leg bend, the path follows a stream fringed by weeping willows. Continue ahead across the car park for Northwick Park sports pavilion, and then down the access road towards the exit. Just before this, take a path to the right skirting the edge of the park. Turn right at the row of trees dividing the field and follow these along the far side. There is a good view to the left of Harrow-on-the-Hill, dominated by St. Mary's church.

At the top of the row of trees turn left, skirting the edge of the field. About halfway along walk through a gap in the hedge. Take the left fork and walk along a grassy path (not very clearly defined) to Watford Road. Turn right here and walk along Watford Road to the pelican crossing in front of the hospital. Cross over and enter Harrow School playing fields signposted Public Footpath to Harrow-on-the-Hill.

Walk along until you reach three signposts, just before a pavilion on the right. Take the left turn signposted Pebworth Road. Walk straight ahead between the rugby pitches and turn left at the end, then almost immediately right to follow a fence and line of trees on your left. At the end of a pitch, and fence, turn right, following the side of the pitch and then turn left to cross over the stile. Keeping the fence on your right, walk straight ahead and cross over a muddy path and then another stile. Keep straight ahead, following a line of small trees on your left. Go through a kissing gate, and walk straight along a fenced path through a second kissing gate. Following the path ahead with a line of trees on your right, you are passing Harrow School Farm. Leave the field by the stile at the end and go along a fenced footpath which emerges onto Pebworth Road. Turn right and then take Littleton Road

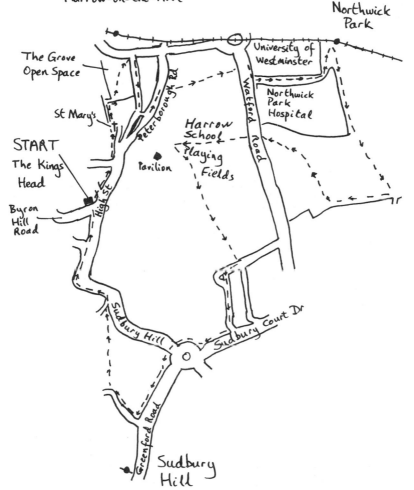

Harrow-on-the-Hill

Northwick Park

The Grove Open Space

University of Westminster

St Mary's

Northwick Park Hospital

Peterborough

Watford Road

Harrow School Playing Fields

START
The Kings Head

Pavilion

Byron Hill Road

High St

Sudbury Hill

Sudbury Court Dr

Greenford Road

Sudbury Hill

to the left, to Sudbury Court Drive, then turn right and follow the road to the roundabout.

Leave by Greenford Road at the opposite side. Just before Sudbury Hill Station (BR), turn right along South Vale, opposite the Rising Sun pub. Just before the barrier, the site of an old toll gate, turn right along a path signposted to Sudbury Hill (Green Lane). At the end turn right onto South Hill Avenue, then at the T junction turn left onto the main road, Sudbury Hill. Walk along here, admiring the large Georgian houses on the right. The road changes its name to London Road and then High Street, where you arrive back at The King's Head.

# 8 Kensal Green
## The Grand Junction Arms

This 200 year old pub (from 1793) was built to serve the Grand Junction Canal. It has its own moorings and canal users still call for refreshment. People walking along the canal also use the pub, and it offers a friendly welcome to a mixed clientele. The large canalside garden is a pleasant sun trap, and has a children's play area. The pub has large, comfortable lounge and public bars (the lounge bar overlooking the canal), and a smaller middle bar. Wearers of outrageous ties, beware, as the landlord may confiscate them to add to his collection pinned up above the lounge bar.

This is a Young's Brewery house, serving Young's Bitter, Special and (part of an old London tradition) Porter from handpumps. Lagers, Guinness and Beamish and Dry Blackthorn Cider are also available on draught. The pub carries a range of about 15 wines in the middle bar.

There is a food servery in the lounge bar, and food is served Monday to Saturday 12 noon – 3 pm and 6 pm – 10 pm, with some cold items being available in the afternoons. A range of sandwiches, rolls and cold items are offered, as well as hot meals such as steak, plaice, gammon, sausage egg and chips, and burgers. A vegetarian dish is usually available. Although no food is served on Sundays, a seafood stall is always parked by the pub entrance, and it is perfectly acceptable to buy food there to eat with your drinks. Children are welcome to accompany their parents for meals, and well-behaved dogs are allowed indoors. The pub is open 11 am – 11 pm Monday to Saturday, and standard Sunday hours. Telephone: 081 965 5670.

*How to get there:* The pub is next to the canal on Acton Lane (B4492), not far from Western Avenue and the North Circular Road. Nearest stations: Harlesden (Bakerloo line/BR) and the walk passes close to Kensal Green (Bakerloo line/BR) and North Acton (Central line).

*Parking:* In the pub car park.

*Length of the walk:* 6¼ miles.

*This is not just a circular but a figure-of-eight walk, featuring prison, death and the North Pole! That may not sound all that appealing, but Kensal Green cemetery is one of the most magnificent in London, full of elaborate monuments to the rich and famous, and the Victorian prison at Wormwood Scrubs is almost a castle. The prison stands next to open parkland from which it takes its name. Much of the walk is along the towpath of the Grand Union Canal, which provides a haven for wildlife even in the middle of industrial wasteland, much of it railway property. The North Pole is the name of the area of BR's freight terminal – not for the Arctic, but for the Channel Tunnel.*

**The Walk**
Leave the pub, turn right, cross the canal, then turn right into Barrets Green Road. Immediately after, take the tarmac path down to the towpath, then turn right to pass the pub and go under Acton Lane bridge. The towpath is initially tarmac, then rather muddy. The canal passes through a power station, the windowless buildings, shuttered bridges and loud humming sounds making an eerie impression. The towpath becomes paved again at the first rail bridge by the power station – power cables now run beneath the paving.

The towpath then becomes slightly elevated for a while, with a thick tangle of plantlife on either side. This provides a good habitat for insects, birds and wild flowers. The overgrown area is then confined to the right of the towpath as it returns to canal level. Go under Old Oak Lane bridge, then the railway bridge and a metal footbridge.

The canal here is quite elevated, giving views to the right over the brick wall of Wormwood Scrubs and the various rail depots. At Mitre Bridge, a metal structure painted blue, red and yellow, leave the towpath by the steps, and turn left onto Scrubs Lane.

Just before the bridge over the railway, turn right into St. Mary's

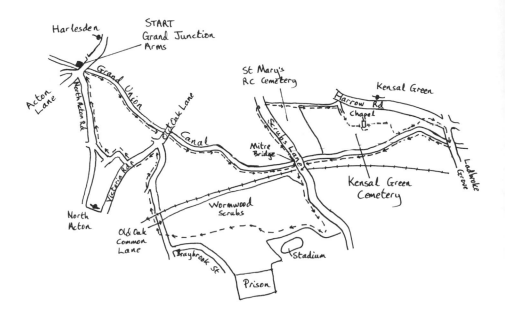

Roman Catholic cemetery though a metal gate. The cemetery is open weekdays 8 am – 5 pm, Sundays 9.15 am – 5 pm in the summer, closing at 4 pm in winter (November – March) and 1 pm on bank holidays, this back gate closing half an hour earlier. Walk straight through St. Mary's cemetery, leaving it by the main gate, and turn right into the grounds of the West London crematorium and Kensal Green cemetery. This is open weekdays 9 am – 6 pm, Sundays 2 pm – 6 pm in summer, closing at sunset in winter (October – March), the gates here closing half an hour earlier. Special opening times apply on bank holidays. Follow the sign 'to the church' to the left, along Oxford Avenue. Kensal Green cemetery was founded in 1832, one of a number to relieve the insanitary overcrowding of the City cemeteries. Many prominent Londoners were buried here, including some members of the Royal family.

Turn left at West Centre Avenue, heading towards the chapel. Go across Cambridge Avenue. The first mausoleum on the left is that of the Duke of Cambridge, a grandson of George III. Shortly after on the right is the grave of Blondin, the tightrope walker. Walk to the right of the chapel, then round in front of it. This simple but impressive building has catacombs below, which may be seen by appointment, or by taking a guided tour of the cemetery, for which there is a fee (starting from here at 11.30 am and 2.30 pm on Saturday, and 2.30 pm on Sundays). Go down the steps in front of the chapel, passing between the two royal tombs. On the left is that of Frederick, Duke of Sussex, 6th son of George III, and on the right Frederick's sister Princess Sophia. Continue along Centre Avenue, passing elaborate family mausolea. Just after a metalled road joins Centre Avenue from the left, turn right down a gravel path towards the fence. A plain white block not far down on the left is the memorial to the Brunel family, including Sir Marc Isambard and his son Isambard Kingdom, the engineers. Continue along this path, crossing another, then turn left near the fence, making for a red brick tomb 34 paces ahead on the left. Next to this is the grave of the novelist William Makepeace Thackeray, the inscription almost illegible.

Continue along this path as it curves round to rejoin Centre Avenue, turn right, and leave the cemetery through the main archway. Turn right, then right again at the crossroads, and cross the canal on Ladbroke Grove. Walk down to the towpath, and continue back towards Mitre Bridge. This section of the towpath is very attractive.

At Mitre Bridge, leave the towpath, and follow Scrubs Lane south to an entrance to Wormwood Scrubs Park. Wormwood means snake-infested wood. Follow the path at the edge of the park, and turn right at the south east corner, where a natural area is fenced off. Follow the fence, then a tarmac path at the end of the fence. Pass the Wormwood Scrubs Park Trim Trail and then the West London Stadium. This is all that remains of the White City, built for the 1908 Olympic Games. Just beyond this, the prison dominates the park. Amongst its celebrated inmates was George Blake, the spy who escaped in 1966.

The park is surprisingly large, accommodating several football pitches, as well as open grasslands. To see more of this, at the edge of the car parks, just before the prison, walk across the park, aiming for the train sheds of Old Oak Common, and a clump of trees and shrubs. Take a path through this, starting near the corner of a football pitch and a park rules notice. After leaving the trees, strike out west across the park. On the right is the long line of sheds for BR's North Pole depot. Pass to the right of some fenced-off clumps of trees, following the line of Braybrook Street. Three policemen were shot dead here in 1966, a crime which shocked the country by its ferocity. Leave what is now Old Oak Common onto Wulfstan Street.

Turn right, go under the railway bridges and follow Old Oak Common Lane past the BR depots, then at the crossroads, turn left onto Victoria Road. Go under the railway bridge, then turn right onto Chandos Road. Follow this to the left at the end, then take the first right (Bashley Road). At the end, turn right onto Chase Road (which becomes North Acton Road). Walk to the crossroads at the end and the pub is on the right over the bridge.

# ⑨ Syon Park
## The London Apprentice

The pub is early 18th century, built on the site of an ancient riverside inn. It was remodelled in 1905 and altered again in the 1960s. The name reflects the fact that London apprentices rowed here from the City on their days off.

There is a good first floor restaurant, and pub food is served from the 'Chef's Fayre' servery on the ground floor. The pub interior is comfortably furnished, and the eating area has a good view of the river, with outdoor terrace seating available. The Chef's Fayre serves food from 12 noon – 2 pm and 7 pm – 9 pm. There is a choice of three or four hot substantial main courses (help yourself to vegetables) and a number of salads. Desserts are served with real cream. Children are welcome in the restaurant and children's helpings are served.

The beers are Ruddles County and Best Bitter and Webster's Yorkshire Bitter. Bottled lagers and wines are also available. Opening times are Monday to Saturday 11 am – 11 pm, and standard Sunday hours. Telephone: 081 560 6136 bar and 081 560 3538 restaurant.

*How to get there:* The pub is at 62 Church Street, Isleworth. From Kew Bridge, take the A315 by the river, passing through Brentford, becoming High Street, then London Road. Take the A310 left at Busch Corner, then turn left onto Park Road, which becomes Church Street. The pub is by the river. Nearest stations: Syon Lane (BR), Kew Bridge (BR), Gunnersbury (BR, District line) – Buses 237 and 267 pass these last two and Syon Park. The walk passes Isleworth (BR). There are admission charges for Syon House and Gardens: a combined ticket costs £4.50 for adults, £3.25 for seniors and juniors; gardens only £2.00/£1.50. (Correct at time of writing.)

*Parking:* Limited by the pub. There is a car park at Syon Park.

*Length of the walk:* 5 miles (inn GR 168761).

*You start in Old Isleworth, and then walk down the Great West Road to experience the history of 20th century industrial architecture. After a brief section on the towpath of the Grand Union Canal, you approach the highlight of the walk, Syon Park and House. Admission is charged for the grounds, which are very well kept and contain some handsome trees. The interior of the house is considered to be one of the finest examples of Robert Adam's work.*

**The Walk**

Leave the pub, turn left and walk along Church Street. At the end is the old Blue School, built in the 18th century and rebuilt as offices in 1983. Turn into Mill Plat, by the old mill stream. On your left pass Ingram's Almshouses (1664).

At the end of the wall on the left, turn left, cross the mill stream (hidden by the wall), then turn right into the park, taking the path following the stream. The narrow strip of land on the other bank is Silverhall Nature Park. Leave the park through the gate and turn left. Pass the end of Sermon's Almshouses (1843) on North Street, and cross Twickenham Road. Turn right onto St. John's Road.

Pass some 1900 villas on the right and then reach the giant Watney Combe Reid brewery on the left. In a pub walk guide, it seems only proper to pass at least one working brewery. Cross the public gardens to the right on a path through the gate near the end of the fence. Then turn left onto Linkfield Road. Pass The Red Lion, with its tiled front, then groups of cottages dating from 1842.

Walk under the railway bridge at London Road by Isleworth station and turn right onto College Road. Turn right into Musgrave Road, then go across Wood Lane into Northumberland Avenue. Continue along this until you reach Gillette Corner on the Great West Road.

When it was being developed in the 1920s and 30s, this was London's Gateway to the West, and it became a showcase of industrial architecture. The tower on the 1937 Gillette building has long been a landmark. Opposite it is the 1987 Sainsbury's Homebase building, with its tower bracing the roof beam, designed by Nicholas Grimshaw (the architect also of the Camden Town Sainsbury's). Cross Syon Lane to walk along the south side of the Great West Road, in front of the Homebase building. On the north side, New Horizon Court (1990-91) follows the yellow-brick road to Post-Modernism. On the south side, No. 941 is a reconditioned 1932 building by Wallis, Gilbert and partners, who designed some of the most outstanding industrial buildings of that time. Their masterpiece, the 1928 Firestone Building (demolished in 1980), was on the north side; all that remains are the white entrance lodges, stone piers in the fence and the 'F' logo in the gates. The glazed replacement behind the gates dates from 1983. Nearly opposite is Westlink House, a surviving 1930 building by Wallis, Gilbert and partners, originally built for Pyrene, and No. 991 (south side) was built in 1935 for Currys by F.E. Simpkins. A common feature of many of these 1930s buildings is the office frontage with a central tower, and a factory behind.

At the bridge over the canal, take the steps to the right down to the towpath, then turn right at the bottom and follow the canal south under the railway bridge and then through a disused warehouse over a wharf. The canal broadens beyond this, where there was once a busy wharf and ends of warehouses on the left overhang the canal for loading and unloading. This is now a bus depot. Go over a small swing bridge, pass Brentford Gauging Lock and reach the end of the canal towpath. Walk up to and cross the main road, pass Brent Lea, then turn left at the path signposted as the pedestrian access to Syon Park.

Pass the entrance to the Heritage Motor Museum and make for the entrance to the grounds and ticket office. What forms the bulk of the present house was built in 1550 and the estate had several changes of owners before the freehold passed to the Percys, Earls of Northumberland. In 1766 the then Earl of Northumberland was created the 1st Duke of Northumberland, and he transformed the estate, commissioning Robert Adam and his brother to reconstruct the interior of the house and Capability Brown to landscape the grounds.

As you enter the grounds, the Great Conservatory is on your right. Turn left onto Conservatory Walk, pass the end of the lake, not taking the lakeside path but walking down the path near the outer perimeter. Walk through the Woodland Gardens and come to Flora's Lawn, in front of a statue of Flora, the goddess of flowers. Continue on round the outer edge of the park, passing the heather banks on the left and an ornamental water garden on the right. Round the corner, passing the end of the lake, then cross the lake via the new metal bridge.

Turn left and follow the lakeside walk back to Conservatory Walk. About half way back, you pass an Indian Bean Tree, spreadeagled over

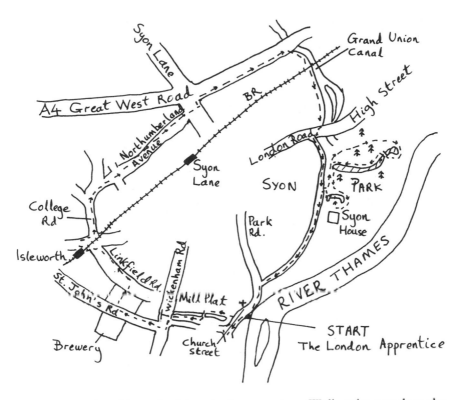

the ground and into the lake. At Conservatory Walk, take a path to the left of the Conservatory and explore the formal garden and the statue of Mercury before entering the Conservatory, built in 1827 by Charles Fowler, who also built the Covent Garden market. Admire the iron pillars and arches under the dome. Leave the conservatory by the left wing to walk through the aquarium, then leave the gardens.

The house entrance is a little further on the left. The original redbrick building was given a stone cladding in the 19th century, but the exterior still has a plain Tudor appearance. In marked contrast, the interior was Robert Adam's first work after returning from Italy in 1762 fresh with inspiration, and he created some of his best work here, particularly in the anteroom. The house is open April to September (and October Sundays), closed on Fridays.

Leave the house and turn left to continue along the road passing through the park. Pass the rose garden then leave the park, turning left onto Park Road to walk through Old Isleworth.

Walk along Church Street, once Isleworth's main thoroughfare, passing 18th century houses and cottages and return to the pub.

43

# 10 Hanwell
## The Fox

The Fox is tucked away out of sight of Hanwell at the end of Green Lane by the canal. It has a peaceful, fair-sized garden (dogs must be on leads) and comfortable unpretentious bars.

The pub has a reputation for its home-cooked food, which is served 12 noon-2 pm, seven days a week. There are occasional barbecues in the summer. The menu changes daily, but usually features a roast, a pie, one or two other dishes such as gammon and pineapple, and a range of filled baguettes and ploughman's lunches. A separate vegetarian menu is also available, with imaginative items such as tagliatelle and nut Wellington. Fresh seasonal vegetables are served wherever possible, lightly cooked to remain firm. Regulars highly recommend the pies, such as steak and kidney, for the pastry as much as the filling. Tempting calorific desserts are available as well as cheese and coffee. Children may eat inside or in the garden.

This is a Courage house, serving Courage Best and Directors ales, Dry Blackthorn Cider and bottled lagers being also available. The opening times are: Monday to Friday 11 am-3 pm, 5.30 pm-11 pm, Saturday 11 am-11 pm, and standard Sunday hours.

Telephone: 081 567 3912.

*How to get there:* The pub is at Green Lane, Hanwell. From Uxbridge Road (A4020) in Hanwell, turn onto Lower Boston Road and then into Green Lane. Nearest stations: Hanwell (BR) with buses 83 and 207 to Hanwell from Ealing Broadway (BR, Central and District lines). Bus E8 passes between Ealing Broadway and Brentford via Boston Manor (Piccadilly line) along Boston Road.

*Parking:* A few spaces in the road by the pub, otherwise try the surrounding streets.

*Length of the walk:* 6¼ miles, or 4½ with a shortcut (inn GR 151796).

*This walk passes along part of the river Brent, giving many opportunities to see wildlife. There is some fine parkland by the river near the Hanwell viaduct, an animal enclosure that will interest children, and the picturesque Hanwell church. After walking along some streets, you visit one of Westminster's cemeteries. A walk through a park, and along the edge of the Brent valley, then a chance to take an attractive short cut or to see Boston Manor and its park, before returning via the canal.*

## The Walk

Leave the pub and go to the canal at the end of Green Lane. Turn right at the towpath, and cross the river Brent. Pass the first lock on the Hanwell flight, and take a footpath to the right, signposted Fitzherbert Walk. This is part of Brent River Park, managed to conserve wildlife and provide interesting walks. Follow the line of the river Brent, ignoring a path to the left. There is much plant growth here, and a well-maintained gravel path. Over to the left are buildings of the Ealing Hospital, with distinctive blue roofs.

Near the water's edge, there is a good mix of trees, shrubs and wild flowers with many types of birds and ducks to be seen. Follow the path under the Uxbridge Road bridge, then go up the steps and turn right into parkland. Ahead of you is Wharncliffe viaduct, built in 1838 by Brunel to carry the main rail line. Follow the path by the Brent towards the viaduct. Cross the river by the bridge at the viaduct, then turn left and go under the viaduct.

Go through the wooden kissing gate and into the park. Turn left onto the path round the perimeter of the park, giving you a good view of the viaduct structure. The path then enters an enclosed garden. A pond on the right with nesting boxes for waterfowl is part of the Brent Lodge Park Animal Centre. To reach the entrance, turn right at the bowling green and approach the cafe. The Animal Centre is divided into a number of enclosures, and has a nominal admission charge. One of its sections is a walled garden containing the wildfowl, and exotic

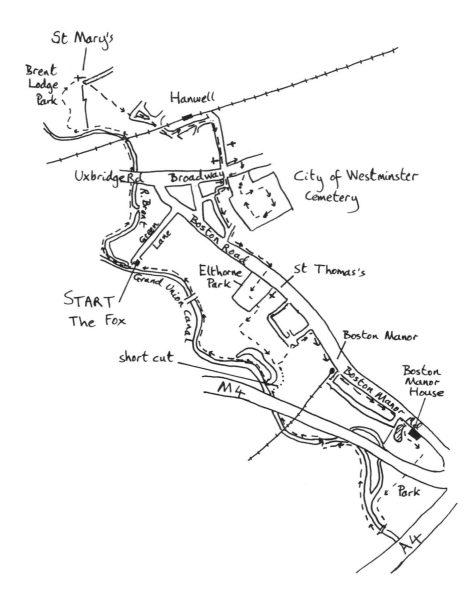

St Mary's

Brent Lodge Park

Hanwell

Uxbridge Rd

Broadway

City of Westminster Cemetery

R. Brent

Green Lane

Boston Road

Elthorne Park

St Thomas's

Boston Manor

START
The Fox

Grand Union Canal

short cut

M4

Boston Manor

Boston Manor House

Park

A4

animals such as wallabies and rheas. Follow the path uphill past the walled garden area, pass the Environmental Centre, and leave the park by the church.

St. Mary's church in Hanwell was built in 1841 by Sir George Gilbert Scott, the architect of St. Pancras station. It has a beautiful position at the end of Churchfields Park, overlooking Brent Lodge Park. Walk past the church, note a group of attractive cottages on the right, and turn half right to take a path through Churchfields Park, between the chestnut trees. To the right of the path, there is a square of chestnut trees surrounding a memorial. This commemorates scouts killed in the two world wars.

As you leave the park, pass the end of Manor Court Road, then turn left into the fenced-in garden and then right to walk through it. This has attractive rose beds and shrubbery. Leave the garden at Alwyne Road, and turn right to take the footpath under the viaduct. On your right is a garden set aside for the aged and blind, and 'others desiring a quiet rest'. Intercity 125 trains thunder past at frequent intervals on the viaduct above.

Turn left into Station Approach (which does not approach the station, the entrance being on Campbell Road), then continue past York Avenue. At the end, turn right into Church Road, then pass Hanwell Methodist church on the left and St. Mellitus church on the right. Ahead, across Broadway is St. Joseph's Roman Catholic church. Turn left along Broadway, and come to the entrance of The City of Westminster cemetery, founded in 1854. This now seems to be open 9 am-4.30 pm throughout the year. A number of mausolea line the approach to the chapels. Beyond the chapels the main monuments of interest commemorate war dead.

Turn left beyond the chapels and walk to the Cross of Sacrifice, commemorating forces dead of the First and Second World Wars, then walk beyond it, turn right and walk between plots 22 and 24, going over a crossroads until you reach plots 21A and 21B on the left. Here there is a mass grave and a memorial to the people of Westminster killed in 1939-1945. Nearby under a tree is a grave for 8 people, apparently from one house, killed by enemy action on the same night in 1941. Walk round the cemetery to return to the chapels, and leave the way you came in.

Turn left onto Broadway, then take the first left, St. George's Road. Turn right into Montague Avenue, then take the second left into Montague Road. Follow this to the end, and turn left onto Boston Road at the Red Lion. Walk along Boston Road, and enter Elthorne Park, on the right, by the main gate. Immediately in front of you, in a circular flower bed, is a 3-ton boulder, which was left at the southern limit of the Ice Age glaciers near what is now Hanwell Station.

Keep straight ahead to the bandstand. The church on the left is St. Thomas's, designed by Edward Maufe, the architect of Guildford cathedral. Pass the bandstand, turn left at the tennis courts, right at the edge of the park, and left to leave the park. Enter a recreation ground, and follow the path to the right round the periphery of the grassland, heading away from the buildings. Turn left at the edge of the flat grassland. The river Brent (made navigable for the canal) is at the bottom of the valley below. There is a good view over the valley and the slope is wild and overgrown. Follow the edge with the football pitches on the left and come to a wooded area.

You can now either take a short cut to the canal towpath, and back to the pub, or continue to see Boston Manor and then return on the towpath.

To take the short cut, take the path through the wood, cross over a stony path and follow a grassy path ahead, skirting the edge of a sports ground. Many birds are to be seen. The path curves round to the right (and may be muddy here) and descends to meet the towpath near the M4, by an arm of the river Brent. Turn right, and skip two paragraphs.

To complete the full walk, do not enter the wood, but walk round the recreation ground and leave it at Wyke Gardens. Walk up Fairfield Road, then turn right onto Boston Road. Pass Boston Manor station, and then shortly come to a corner entrance of Boston Manor Park. Enter the park, and skirt the left of the small lake to reach the back of the house. Boston Manor is a brick 17th century house, having some similarities with Forty Hall in Enfield, bought by the local authority in 1923. It is open to the public only on summer Sunday afternoons. The park is always open, however.

Pass the end of the house, and turn right, taking a path under the M4. There is a nature trail through the natural areas of the park which you may want to follow (signs will guide you), otherwise walk round the edge of the park to reach the canal. There is a footbridge over the canal in the far corner of the park (it's not on most maps, but it is there). Cross the bridge, then follow the towpath with the canal to your right to pass the rear of Boston Manor park. The towpath crosses to the other side at Gallows Bridge. Then you pass under the Piccadilly Line bridge and the M4.

The long route meets the short cut here. Follow the path past Osterley Lock and the weir, and continue on under Bumper's Lane Bridge. Eventually you reach the point where the Brent joins the canal. Leave the towpath just before this, and return to the pub.

# ⑪ Osterley Park
## The Hare and Hounds

The Hare and Hounds is near the entrance to Osterley Park. Built in 1904, it has unpretentious brick and wood decor, a dartboard with electronic scoring, and several certificates for good cellar management proudly displayed. There is a fairly large garden, with a play area.

This is a popular Fuller's pub, serving Fuller's London Pride and ESB from handpumps, Chiswick Bitter, Chiswick Mild and Strongbow Cider being also on draught. Bottled premium lagers are available. A range of pub food is served seven days a week, ranging from salads, sandwiches and ploughman's lunches, to a choice of several hot main courses, such as casseroles, pies and fish, followed by desserts, all at reasonable prices. A roast lunch is served on Sundays. Food is served every day from 12 noon – 2.30 pm and 5 pm – 9.30 pm (Sunday evening 7 pm – 9 pm). Children may join their parents for meals.

Opening times are Monday to Friday 11.30 am – 3 pm, 5 pm – 11 pm, Saturday 11.30 am – 11 pm and Sunday 12 noon – 3 pm, 7 pm – 10.30 pm. Telephone: 081 560 5438.

*How to get there:* The pub is on Windmill Lane next to the garden centre near the start of Syon Lane (this is all the B454), which comes northwards off the A4. Nearest stations: Osterley (Piccadilly line) and Syon Lane (BR).

*Parking:* In the pub car park and there is a car park in Osterley Park (free to NT members, otherwise fee).

*Length of the walk:* 3¼ miles (inn GR 158783).

*Osterley House is a gem. The exterior and interior, nearly all the work of Robert Adam, form a single architectural unit. Adam designed everything down to the keyhole covers, and nearly all of his interior work on the house has been retained over the years. This walk is a very pleasant stroll, with no stile or hills to climb, almost entirely within the National Trust parkland surrounding the house, all very sensitively maintained. The park contains some magnificent trees and much birdlife.*

## The Walk

Leave the pub, turn left and cross the road, taking care. Take a path half right following the edge of the green towards the lodges at the entrance to Osterley Park, then turn right onto the gravel drive passing between them. This entrance is only for pedestrians, the vehicle entrance being on Jersey Road. The park is open all year from 9 am – 7.30 pm or dusk if earlier, free to all. The house is open April to October 1 pm – 5 pm Wednesday – Saturday, 11 am – 5 pm Sundays and bank holiday Mondays, free to NT members, otherwise admission charge. If your dog is with you, one of you should read the rules about where dogs should be on leads or excluded from.

Walk up the drive, Osterley Lane, a public road until the late 19th century. The lane passes between fields containing horses (please do not feed them) and then two lakes. Look over Middle Lake to the left to get your first view of the magnificent front of Osterley House.

After passing the lake, Osterley Lane curves to the left at the M4, which bisects the original estate. Just past this bend, go through a wicket gate in the fence on the left (if you want to visit the house without risking muddy feet, keep straight on then turn left at the entrance by the avenue). Take a path to the right following the bank of Middle Lake. On the left is an island acting as a refuge for birds, particularly herons, that are not overeager to meet humans. Follow the bank round to the left and then the right.

The house is presented to you across the parkland. Follow the lake through a clump of trees and come out onto the approach road to the house. Turn right, and follow the curve, passing the stable block, built in the 1570s and altered by successive owners, housing the tea room on the right.

Now approach the house. The original building was a red brick Tudor mansion enclosing three sides of a courtyard, completed in 1575 for Sir Thomas Gresham, who founded the Royal Exchange. The estate was purchased by the Child family in 1711, and from 1756 they

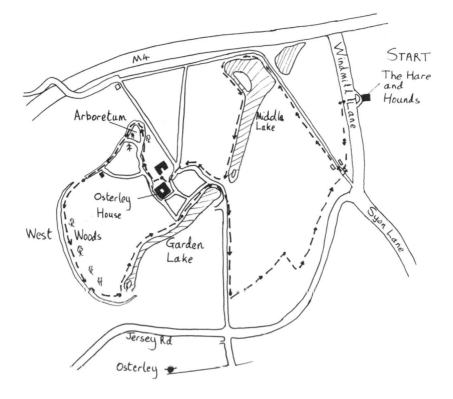

commissioned first Sir William Chambers (architect of Somerset House and the Kew pagoda), then his fellow Scot, Robert Adam, to transform the house. Chambers soon gave up the commisson, and most of what you see is due to Adam, whose masterpiece is the classical screen of pillars with which he closed the fourth side of the courtyard, and which makes a magnificent entrance. The house remained in the Child family until 1949, when it was given to the nation. It is probably thanks to this uninterrupted ownership that so much of Adam's interior work has been retained, and that the building and furnishings form a stylistic whole.

After visiting the house, turn left and left again to pass between the house and stable block, then turn right, following the wall of the stable block, admiring the Magnolia grandiflora growing against it. Fork right to pass in front of the semicircular Robert Adam Garden House (once used as an aviary). This part of the gardens is the Pleasure Grounds. There was an orangery here, but it burned down in 1950.

Turn right into the Pinetum and Arboretum, following the path

51

along the walled garden (to which there is no public access). Do not leave the garden at the exit onto the avenue, but turn sharp left and follow the path back into the Arboretum. Pass the end of a path flanked by two giant cedars leading back to the walled garden, keeping straight on. Ahead is the Temple of Pan (Chambers), used by the family for picnics and study. Go straight on past this, and then past a cottage on the right. You now have a view of fields to the right, over the fence. To your left is the Great Meadow, once enclosed and grazed, now parkland. Keep following the path round the outer periphery of the estate into West Woods.

This is a good place to see some of the birdlife associated with the estate: nuthatches, treecreepers and long-tailed tits are common, and you will often at least hear woodpeckers. The West Woods contain some exotic trees, such as Hungarian oaks, North American Red and Scarlet oaks and rhododendrons. The native trees are yews, beeches and oaks. The woods are now actively managed to repair storm damage, and to provide some younger trees, shrubs and woodland plants. As you walk round the outer perimeter, you come to a T junction, a fence ahead barring access to a small island in Garden Lake. Turn left, then almost immediately right onto the next path, following the line of the fence and then the lake.

From here, you get a good view of the west front of the house, which is part of the work by Chambers. Pass two ancient oaks on small mounds, then skirt a much larger mound, marking the site of an icehouse, which was filled during 1939. You now get a better view of Garden Lake and the side of the house, with Cedar Lawn in between. Luckily, these magnificent cedars were relatively undamaged in the storms of 1987 and 1990.

Chambers was a great enthusiast for Chinese style and the house itself has a number of Chinese artefacts, especially in the Long Gallery, one of the few internal parts that Chambers designed, and you see a Chinese pavilion at the end of the lake. This is new (1987), donated by a Hong Kong businessman, and is a copy of the pavilion by Chambers in the Menagerie Lake at Kew.

At the end of the lake, turn right and follow the road past the car park. Pass a bungalow on the left 'Osterley Park Veg Farm', which may be selling fresh produce, then a little further on, turn left (opposite another bungalow) through a kissing gate onto a fenced path between two fields. A line of trees marks the path. On the right there is open meadow, on the left parkland and trees. At a metal kissing gate the path turns right 90° to run towards the houses, then left 90° next to them, and runs along the edge of the field. This eventually emerges onto the green in front of the lodges. Retrace your steps to the pub.

# ⑫ Ruislip
## The Six Bells

The Six Bells is a Taylor Walker house with a wonderful position on the edge of Mad Bess Wood. The building is over 300 years old, but has only been used as a pub for about the last century, having been said to have found use as magistrates' court and a morgue before that. There is, however, little trace of these earlier uses. The pub has two small, intimate bar areas with flagstone floors and wooden beams.

It is preferred that children stay in the garden area, but there are unlikely to be many protests as this is a major feature, with many benches and tables, some under cover, a large lawn and trees, climbing frames and slides and a skittles alley protected from the rain. The pub serves simple bar meals seven days a week. Toasted sandwiches, pies, burgers and pizzas are available during opening hours, which are Monday to Saturday 11 am-11 pm and Sunday 12 noon-3 pm, 7 pm-10.30 pm.

Tetley Bitter, Wadworth 6X, Young's, Benskins and Burton Ale are available on handpump, and Merrydown Cider is on draught. Customers' dogs are welcome.

Telephone: 0895 639466.

*How to get there:* The pub is on Duck's Hill Road. Leaving Ruislip northwards on the A4180 towards the lido, pass Breakspear Road on the left, then the fire station. This is now Duck's Hill Road, and the pub is on the left, just after Reservoir Road (the turn off to the right for the lido). Nearest Underground station: Ruislip (Metropolitan line with buses from station to Ruislip Lido).

*Parking:* You are very welcome to leave your car in the pub car park while you walk, but please tell the manager or one of the bar staff, so that they know to whom the car belongs.

*Length of the walk:* 3¼ miles (inn GR 083891).

*A pleasant stroll, with a few gentle slopes, through the woods surrounding Ruislip Lido, Park Wood, Copse Wood and Mad Bess Wood. The trees and the closeness of the water provide a rich wildlife habitat (be prepared for some areas to be wet underfoot).*

## The Walk

Leaving the pub, turn right onto Duck's Hill Road, passing the fire station on the right. The road is renamed Bury Street. Continue past Breakspear Road, passing the attractive and well-preserved old brick and timber farmhouse of Cannon's Bridge Farm on the left. When the wooden fence round this property ends, turn left onto a track leading into Park Wood. Follow this a short way, then go straight across the first crossroads you come to, taking the footpath heading uphill. This leads through a mixed broadleaf wood. There are occasional glimpses to the left of the lido. You come to a relatively open area where about five paths meet. Make a 90° turn to the left here and walk downhill. You shortly come to the rear exit of the lido (exit only, no entrance), near the start of the miniature railway. Turn right and follow the fence.

Ruislip Lido was originally a reservoir built as a feeder for the Grand Union Canal, but later became a very popular site for water-related recreation. Sadly, at the moment, although the word lido means an open air bathing pool, no swimming is permitted, as a very low water level makes this unsafe. Water skiing and boating still take place, however, the lido has an increasingly popular picnic area, and the miniature railway has recently been extended.

As you approach the end of the lake the path crosses a plank bridge and starts to climb, becoming gravelled. Come out of the wood onto the border of the golf course, keeping to the path, which re-enters the trees. When you come to a fork in the path by a small derelict building, keep straight on, ignoring the left fork. Eventually the trees thin out, and you are on a path at the edge of Haste Hill municipal golf

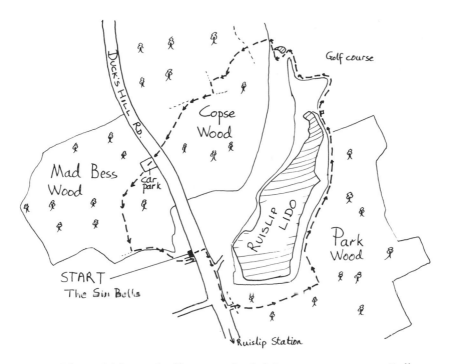

course. The wild fenced-off area to the left is a nature reserve. Follow the fence round a 90° bend to the left and enter the trees again.

At a T junction signposted Public Footpath in each direction, turn left, and cross the stream over a concrete bridge. You are now walking through a rich wildlife habitat of streams, undergrowth, shrubbery and trees. Turn left at a crossroads with another path, and cross over a muddy pond using the bridge across the end. The landscape changes here and an open grassy area borders on the pond. This area is known as Poor's Field, and is adjacent to Ruislip Common. Keep an eye open for dragonflies near the pond. When you reach another path, turn right onto it, cross a concrete bridge at the other end of the pond, and immediately turn left 90° into Copse Wood.

Ignoring a path to the half right, go straight across a better-defined path and then turn half right onto a well-defined bridlepath. Take the first narrow path leading off to the left through the woods. Very shortly, this leads across a narrow stream (no bridge!). Keep following this path until you come to a very obvious straight gravel track with a ditch by the side. Turn right onto this, and walk uphill. The wood becomes more open, with birch and beech trees to the right, and dense undergrowth to the left. Much birdlife is in evidence.

At a T junction, turn left, continuing to climb (you should be heading south here). Turn right at the next T junction, heading roughly west. Pass a small marker post on the right marked '16' (and with an arrow pointing back the way you came). This path is in a broad lane through the trees at first, then it swings away to the left into the wood, through an area overgrown by bracken. Follow this path round to an exit from the wood over a stile onto Duck's Hill Road.

Cross this busy road with care and follow the public footpath sign into the car park opposite. Walk across the car park, and leave it via the left hand corner on a path leading away to the half left into Mad Bess Wood. This is said to be named after an old woman who lived in the wood, but no humans seem to be in residence now.

You should be heading nearly south. The path descends and veers round to the right. Cross a plank bridge over a ditch by a straight gravel track, and go across the track onto a footpath heading approximately south south west. Cross another ditch and turn left at a T junction onto a broad path. Take the left fork where two broad paths diverge.

Go straight across a crossroads of broad paths, and come to a T junction near the edge of the wood, signposted Public Footpath in each direction. Turn left to follow the edge of the wood and the crematorium area on the right. Cross a stile onto a private road. The pub is at the end on the left, by the main road.

# 13 Twickenham
## The Barmy Arms

The Barmy Arms was established in 1727 as the Queen's Head, but over the years came to be known as the 'Barmy Arms' and locals will tell you that this name referred to one of the early landlords who was renowned for his barminess. The mundane explanation that it referred to the froth on top of fermenting ale is more likely, 'barmy' being an old name for frothy.

There are a number of tables outside where you can eat peacefully facing the river (The Embankment here is pedestrianised), and the pub has a separate restaurant, open at lunchtimes, where children are welcome – they are not allowed in the bar. Food is served seven days a week, Monday to Saturday 12 noon-2 pm and Sunday 12.30 pm-2.30 pm, a choice of about ten main courses being available, as well as sandwiches and ploughman's, and desserts to satisfy the sweet tooths amongst you. Bar food is available in the evenings, 7 pm-9 pm.

This is a Watney's house, and the beers served are Webster's Yorkshire Bitter, Ruddles County and Ruddles Best. Woodpecker Cider is on draught, and bottled lagers are available.

The pub is open Monday to Saturday 11 am-11 pm in summer and 11 am-3 pm and 5.30 pm-11 pm in winter, Sundays 12 noon-3 pm and 7 pm-10.30 pm. Telephone: 081 892 0863.

57

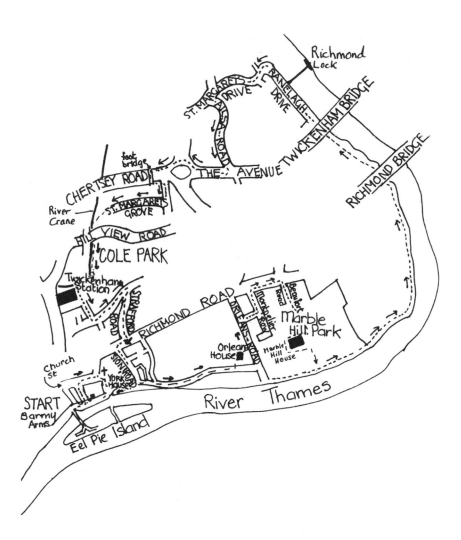

*How to get there:* The pub is on The Embankment at Twickenham, opposite Eel Pie Island. Nearest stations: Twickenham (BR) and part of the walk is near Richmond (District line and BR).

*Parking:* No pub car park, but there is a public car park in front accessible from King Street (A310) via Water Lane. This is free on Sundays and Public Holidays, hourly charge Monday to Friday.

*Length of the walk:* 4½ miles.

*Twickenham is a London riverside village with a distinctive nautical feel to it. Many of its 17th and 18th century mansions survive and some of them are open to the public. This walk explores the grounds of three of them — all very different — and goes along one of the most attractive sections of the Thames towpath, from where there are fine views of Richmond.*

## The Walk

Leave the pub, turn right and take the footbridge on the left to Eel Pie Island. From the bridge there is a splendid view downriver. The island's name derives from Victorian times when a tavern there sold eel pies to daytrippers who came here by boat from London. The pies and the tavern are no more, the latter ending its days as a hippy squat in the 60s. The Rolling Stones, amongst others, played there then. Later it was demolished and replaced with characterless town houses. Now the island is an unattractive hotchpotch of these houses, wooden chalets and boatyards. The two main paths on the island are both cul-de-sacs making a circular walk around the island impossible.

Return to The Embankment, turn right and then left onto Bell Lane and then right onto Church Street. Walk to the end here and enter St. Mary-the-Virgin churchyard. The original church was built in 1332 and rebuilt in the late 14th century. Leave the churchyard, turn left, walk down Church Lane, then turn left into Riverside. Go under two footbridges and enter Orleans House through the gateway on the left.

Orleans House was built by John James in 1710 for James Johnstone, who had been William III's Secretary of State for Scotland. It was named Orleans in the early 19th century when Louis-Philippe, Duc d'Orleans (and future king of France) lived there. Sadly, most of the house was demolished in 1926 by William Cunard the shipping entrepreneur, but the octagon pavilion added by Johnstone in 1720 remains. The pavilion — now the Orleans House Gallery — is open to the public Tuesday-Saturday 1 pm-5.30 pm April-October, closing one hour earlier October-March, admission free.

On leaving the gallery, walk past the Octagon and go straight ahead through the gardens in front, which lead to an exit. Turn left onto Orleans Road, right onto Chapel Road and then left onto Montpelier Row which is one of outer London's finest Georgian terraces.

At the top turn right onto Richmond Road, walk along here and turn right into Beaufort Road, leading to the main entrance into Marble Hill Park. Once in the park walk straight ahead and then take the path to the right signposted Clockhouse and Restaurant to find Marble Hill House on the left along here. This was built in the Palladian style by Roger Morris in 1723 for Henrietta Howard, later Countess of Suffolk, the mistress of George II. It is open daily 10 am-6 pm from Good Friday or 1st April (whichever comes earlier) until 1st October, then

10 am-4 pm the rest of the year, admission free.

On leaving the house turn left and then first left again, thus walking round the house and the immediate fenced-in (semi-wilderness) area. To the right a path leads to The Grotto, designed by Pope in the 1740s. Continue to the main path, turn right to walk to the river, leave the park, and turn left at the riverside.

Now walk along this attractive riverside path. Continue over into Willoughby Road followed by Duck's Walk. Walk under Richmond Railway Bridge. Continue straight ahead along Ranelagh Drive by the river, passing the wonderful Richmond half-tide weir and footbridge.

The road curves round to the left, becoming St. Margaret's Drive. This is St. Margaret's Estate, begun in 1854 in the grounds of St. Margaret's House (now the West London Institute). This was built up slowly, leaving parts of the grounds as pleasure gardens, two of which you skirt as you continue round. Turn left into Ailsa Road; No. 46 (built 1935) is a striking Modern Movement insertion. Continue to the end of this road and turn right onto The Avenue, cross St. Margaret's Road then cross Chertsey Road by the footbridge.

Walk back along Chertsey Road and turn right into Winchester Road. Take the first right at the Turks Head pub into St. Margaret's Grove. Continue along the footpath straight ahead, approaching the canalised river Crane. Just beyond the children's playground turn right and leave the park via the bridge over the Crane.

Turn left into Cole Park Road and take the first footpath to the left. Cross the bridge over the Crane, then the footbridge by Twickenham station. Continue straight ahead along Beauchamp Road, turn left at the end into Amyand Park Road, pass the end of Oak Lane and turn right into Strafford Road. At the end cross Richmond Road, walk along Sion Road, and enter York House grounds on the right.

York House's present function as municipal offices contrasts with its grander past. It was built in the mid 17th century, as a summer residence for the Earl of Clarendon, Lord Chancellor to Charles II. The last private resident was the Indian tycoon Sir Ratan Tata. The house is only open for guided tours during Twickenham week but the grounds are open daily, admission free. Walk to the rear of the house, turn left and pass the sunken lawn on the right. Beyond the lawn cross the stone footbridge, turn left and walk through the rose garden. Turn right and at the waterfront turn right again, then take the first right and then left to reach a fountain bedecked with seven voluptuous nude nymphs, this extraordinarily elaborate creation having been installed by Sir Ratan. At the fountain turn left, leave the garden through the gate in the wall and the Barmy Arms is in front of you.

# Chiswick
## The City Barge

This riverside pub, originally called the Navigator's Arms, was built in 1484. It changed its name to the present one in the 19th century supposedly because the Lord Mayor's barge moored here. It suffered badly from bomb damage in the Second World War so consequently is largely rebuilt. The steel door leading to the old bar is needed when the Thames runs high in front of the pub.

The pub has a cosy intimate atmosphere, and serves excellent food seven days a week. There is a good choice of tasty dishes with at least two vegetarian dishes daily, a roast on Sundays and a range of desserts is available. This is a Courage house and has Courage Best, Directors Bitter and John Smith's on handpump. Scrumpy Jack and Strongbow ciders are on draught. Children can join their parents for meals, especially in the conservatory area – in the evening until 9 pm. There are benches outside for good weather, giving a good view over the river.

The pub is open 12 noon-11 pm Monday-Saturday and 12 noon-3 pm and 7 pm-10.30 pm Sunday. Food is served 12 noon-2.30 pm and 7 pm-9 pm Monday-Saturday, and 12 noon-2 pm Sunday.

Telephone: 081 994 2148.

61

*How to get there:* The pub is at 27 Strand-on-the-Green, which comes off Kew Bridge Road (A205) on the northern bank of the river. The pub is near the railway bridge. Nearest stations: Kew Bridge (BR), Gunnersbury (District line).

*Parking:* Pub car park is off Thames Road. Spaces for 12-15 cars. You can leave your car there during the walk as long as you're not blocking anyone. Otherwise, spaces along surrounding streets.

*Length of the walk:* 5 miles.

*The walk begins by going along the towpath at Strand-on-the-Green, which is one of London's most picturesque villages. The name derives from an orchard which used to be at the back of the houses. The well-preserved houses are almost all 18th century. The walk continues on to Hogarth's House and the magnificent Palladian Revival villa in Chiswick Park.*

**The Walk**

Leave the pub, turning left onto the towpath to head under the railway bridge. Near the Bull's Head are some 18th century cottages built for the 'use of the poor of Chiswick for ever'. Over to the right, on the other side of the river, you can just see the top of the Public Record Office building at Kew.

When Strand-on-the-Green comes to an end, follow Grove Park Road and then Hartington Road to Chiswick Bridge. Take the subway, then follow the path round the back of Guy's Hospital boat club. You are now on a tarmac road, with a grass verge on the right by the river. Go past the Stag brewery on the opposite bank, and then a riverside footpath starts after a small car park. Follow this path round the edge of Duke's Meadows until it ends at Chiswick boat house, just before Barnes Bridge, a rail and foot bridge. Turn left onto a tarmac road following the railway line, go through the bridge under the railway, then turn right and continue along the road which becomes a narrow tarmac path. Walk to the end of this path and turn left at the river. Pass the boathouse of Emanuel School boat club. There are good views of Barnes on the opposite side of the river.

The path eventually veers off to the left away from the river, becoming a private road. Walk to the end of this and, at the crossroads, take the right turn into Pumping Station Road, skirting Chiswick cemetery. Follow this road to the end and proceed along the footpath with Chiswick parish church (St. Nicholas) on the left. Go up the steps to the churchyard and on the left is William Hogarth's grave (d. 1764 aged 67), a large monument surrounded by railings. Whistler is also buried here, near Hogarth, as are two of Cromwell's daughters

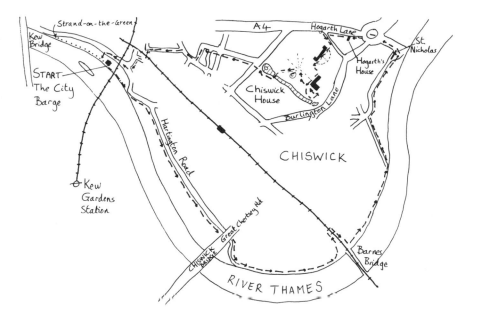

(there is even a story that Cromwell's remains were reburied here after being exhumed and publicly mutilated during the restoration). Leave the churchyard and go up Church Street (left from the river). Go under the subway, take the left turn in the subway (look out for the blue tiles), turn right at the end and at the top of the steps walk straight ahead along Hogarth Lane to reach Hogarth's House on the left.

This house (built 1700) was owned by Hogarth between 1749 and 1764, and is now open to the public. (Monday and Wednesday to Saturday 11 am-6 pm summer, 11 am-4 pm winter, Sunday 2 pm-6 pm summer, 2 pm-4 pm winter; closed Tuesdays and the first two weeks in September). The house has narrow steep stairs, and wood-panelled rooms which contain a large collection of Hogarth's engravings.

Turn left out of Hogarth's House to continue along Hogarth Lane, then turn left through a gateway onto Duke's Avenue, to visit Chiswick House and Park. Just over halfway down the Avenue, turn right at a signpost to the Interpretive Centre. Walk through the formal Italian Garden, following the front of the Conservatory. Leave the garden via the box hedge and topiary, and turn left at the ha-ha (sunken fence). Turn right at the Inigo Jones Gateway (built in 1621, and erected here in 1738). Walk past the back of the house to the lake, then look back to admire the house, which was designed and built in the Palladian style by its owner, Richard Boyle, 3rd Earl of Burlington, in 1725-1729. Lord Burlington was an admirer of Inigo Jones and the Italian architect Palladio, whose buildings he had studied in Italy. Lord Burlington originally built the house as a villa linked to his Jacobean mansion (demolished 1788), not to live in but to exhibit his collection of pictures and sculptures.

The house was extensively restored in 1929 (a succeeding Duke of Devonshire – Burlington's only child, a daughter, married the 4th Duke – had leased it out as a private lunatic asylum) and now closely resembles its original state. The house is open 15 March-15 October 9.30 am-6.30 pm, and 16 October-14 March 9.30 am-4 pm, admission charge. The grounds are open from 8 am to dusk, admission free.

To get to the entrance of the house, walk first to the end of the lake to see the cascade, then cross the lawn to the door at the front (at ground level). When you leave the house, walk round to the back, then away from the house taking the path following the avenue of trees and the statuary. The gardens were laid out in 1730-1740, by William Kent, an architect, designer and painter whom Burlington met in Italy. This section of the garden contains some magnificent cedars of Lebanon. Part of Kent's design for the garden was a system of walkways and avenues radiating from a 'patte d'oie' (goose foot, from the shape made by the paths) and terminating in classical buildings. Turn left at the patte d'oie you are now approaching to take the path past the amphitheatre and the stone monument with a Latin inscription marking the grave of Lilly, a faithful dog.

Cross the lake at the Classic bridge, then turn right and follow the path to the end of the lake and leave the grounds via the gateway onto Park Road. Turn right then immediately left onto Chesterfield Road.

You will now walk through some quiet suburban streets having a variety of brick housing. Go straight across Sutton Court Road into Sutton Court. Sutton Court Mansions were built in 1906 on the site of the old manor house. At the end of the flats on the right, turn left into Compton Crescent, then at the end of this, turn right onto Fauconberg Crescent (one of Cromwell's daughters buried in Chiswick churchyard was Mary, Lady Fauconberg). Notice the remnants of a former icehouse (from the old manor house?) at the corner of Grove Park Terrace.

Turn left off Fauconberg Road onto Gordon Road, then at the end turn left into Deans Close, continuing into Deans Lane and follow the footpath over the railway footbridge into Herbert Gardens, turning left at the end into Magnolia Road. Turn right into Thames Road, go under the railway, pass the back of the pub then, just next to it, turn left into Post Office Alley, which was featured in the Beatles film *Help*. This leads back to Strand-on-the-Green and you turn left to return to the pub.

# 15 Stanmore Hill
## The Vine

The Vine has an attractive position in the Little Common conservation area at the top of Stanmore Hill. Inside, there is a pleasing amount of dark wood furniture and half-panelling, supplemented with the currently fashionable display of ageing bric-a-brac, such as old suitcases, household implements, lamps and so on. Dogs may be brought inside, if kept away from the eating area.

Good, reasonably-priced food is served seven days a week in a separate room off the lounge bar and children are welcome there. Grilled steaks are a featured speciality; the menu includes a wide range of starters followed by meat, fish, and two vegetarian main courses, together with cold dishes and desserts, and is served at lunchtime from 12 noon to 2 pm every day (last order 1.50 pm) and in the evenings from 6.30 pm (7 pm on Sundays) to 9 pm.

Beers served in this Benskins house are Benskins Best Bitter, Ind Coope Burton Ale and Tetley Bitter. Draught Old English Cider is served, and some bottled lagers and wines are also available. Outside, there is a beer garden where children are also welcome.

Opening times are Monday-Friday 11 am-3 pm, 5 pm-11 pm, Saturday 11 am-3 pm, 6 pm-11 pm, Sunday 12 noon-3 pm, 7 pm-10.30 pm. Telephone: 081 954 4676.

*How to get there:* The Vine is at the top of Stanmore Hill (just before it becomes The Common), No. 173 opposite Hill House – this is the A4140 leading north out of Stanmore. Nearest Underground station: Stanmore (end of the Jubilee line). The pub is on bus route 142, and Uxbridge Road, part of which is on the walk, is served by buses H12 and 340.

*Parking:* Small pub car park.

*Length of the walk:* 4¼ miles (inn GR 163931).

*This is a predominantly rural walk near Bentley Priory with some fine views of London. Stanmore means 'stoney mere' and mere being an ancient word for pond this presumably refers to the ponds at the top of Stanmore Hill. Near the beginning of the walk there is an opportunity to explore the ruins of Great Stanmore old church, described by Pevsner as one of the best ruins in Middlesex.*

## The Walk

Leave the pub, turn left and go down Stanmore Hill. A little way along here on the left, just beyond Wood Lane, is Stanmore Hall. This was built in 1843 and extended in 1890 when the interior was refurbished by William Morris and Edward Burne-Jones. It was redeveloped into offices following a fire in 1979. Cross the road here, admire the view to the south over London as you walk downhill, and a little further on fork right into Green Lane. You pass many attractive cottages as you walk down.

At the end of Green Lane, cross over Uxbridge Road. Ahead of you

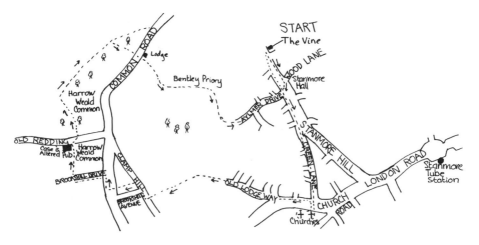

are the old and new parish churches of St. John the Evangelist. Great Stanmore old church, built in 1632 of red brick, was abandoned as unsafe around 1845, and was left to become a ruin. While the ruin was being made safe to mark its 360th anniversary in 1992, a Victorian mystery was solved. The coffin of Lord Aberdeen, prime minister at the start of the Crimean War, and who died in 1860, was found when the family vault was rediscovered. Also in the vault were the coffins of the earl's two wives and three of his daughters, all of whom died prematurely. When the earl died, the old church was already a ruin, but he wished to be buried with the rest of his family. The location of the vault, the grave of this prime minister who was called a faithful friend of Queen Victoria, was then forgotten. It is now marked with a plaque unveiled by the present Marquess of Aberdeen in July 1992.

Next to the ruin is the new church, built in 1850. This contains many of the monuments from the old church. Leave the churchyard by the lychgate, turn left and walk along Uxbridge Road. Pass RAF Stanmore Park, with its Gloster Javelin gate guardian. Cross over here and a little further along turn right onto Old Lodge Way. Follow the road round and at the end go through the wooden kissing gate, one of the starting points of the Bentley Priory Circular Walk, which goes through the most attractive parts of Harrow's green belt.

Just beyond the gate, a notice board gives information about the walk. Take the tarmac path straight ahead and at the first signpost take the left turning indicated to Clamp Hill onto a grassy path. The path goes across open grassland and then through a short stretch of woodland. Go through the kissing gate and over the wooden bridge across a stream, then take the path to the right following a ditch. Cross the end of a cul-de-sac and follow the narrow path straight ahead, through a canopy of trees where you will have the opportunity to see some of the birds mentioned on the notice board. Go through a kissing gate onto a wider track with a school playing field on the left.

The track emerges on Clamp Hill. Turn right here, cross the road, ignore a footpath sign pointing down Brookshill Avenue, and just beyond this turn left onto a path signposted Brookshill and Circular Walk. This path is easily missed, but it is marked on the right of the road by a wooden post with a yellow arrow, and is just past Brickfield Cottage. At the end of this footpath a yellow arrow shows a right turn onto Brookshill.

Cross the road and then turn left onto Brookshill Drive signposted Old Redding and Circular Walk. At Copse Farm bear right and follow the signposted footpath to Old Redding. There are some fine 18th century cottages on the right and on the left are rolling hills, trees and views of Northwood. Harrow-on-the-Hill is to the south behind you.

On the left at the end of the path is The Case is Altered pub, this name being a corruption of Casa Alta (High House). On the far side of the pub is a public car park and a viewpoint. Just west of here is Grims Dyke which originated as a fortification for a Saxon camp.

Turn right onto Old Redding and enter Harrow Weald Common on the left. Weald is an old English word for forest, and Harrow Weald was part of the old Forest of Middlesex, first mentioned in 1303. It was a favourite haunt of highwaymen in the 18th century. Nuthatches and green woodpeckers may be spotted here. Follow the track straight ahead through the wood ignoring the bridlepath marked by white posts to the right and continue along the track to a group of half-timbered cottages on the left. Follow a yellow arrow past these and then more houses and open fields on the left. Re-enter the wood at the end of the field, then look out for a yellow arrow pointing to the right, and follow it. The path is indistinct here so do not be led astray by a path to the left with a bench by it, but keep going up to the road. Steps lead up to Common Road.

Cross the road and go through the wooden barred gate opposite (next to the lodge – a yellow arrow beyond the gate confirms the route) into Bentley Priory grounds and along the narrow wooded path straight ahead. At the end of this path go through the kissing gate and take the concrete path veering diagonally left. This path skirts the south edge of Bentley Priory grounds.

Bentley Priory was founded around 1170, and was suppressed in the Reformation. A house was built on the site in 1766, and this was enlarged in 1790 by Sir John Soane (architect of the Bank of England). William IV's widow queen Adelaide used the house, and died here in 1849. It became the property of the Air Ministry in 1925 and RAF Fighter Command HQ. The Battle of Britain was controlled from here.

As the serious-looking barbed wire boundary fence implies,there is no public admission to the house. There is a good view to the right of the extensive open space and City of London. You get fleeting glimpses of the house and its clocktower, especially near the radio mast. At the next signpost turn right onto a broader tarmac path signposted Stanmore Church. On the left is a fenced-in deer park containing fallow deer. There is a nature reserve in the centre of the open space over to the right (no public access). Just beyond the fence take a path to the left indicated by a wooden post with a yellow arrow, then go up the steps and through the kissing gate to emerge onto Aylmer Drive.

Walk along here passing Adelaide Close on the right. Continue straight ahead to Stanmore Hill, turn left and The Vine is ahead of you on the right.

# 16 Welsh Harp
## The White Lion of Mortimer

This is an enormous free house, one of the Wetherspoons chain, specialising in carrying a good range of real ales. As it is a pub on a city street, there is no garden or admission to children or dogs, so save it for an adults-only walk, but it is very popular with an otherwise mixed clientele, and can get quite busy at lunchtimes and evenings. Although it was established in 1989, The White Lion of Mortimer has been decorated to resemble a traditional city centre pub with wooden and glass screens, wrought ironwork and chandeliers. There are comfortable chairs and sofas to lounge in, tables and chairs, and an open-plan first floor dining area (open lunchtimes and evenings) reached by a spiral staircase.

A good range of tasty food is served seven days a week, with the hours being Monday – Saturday 11 am – 10 pm, Sunday 12 noon – 2.30 pm. The menu ranges from ploughman's lunches and pies to house specialities such as beef cobbler (cooked in Theakstons XB with a scone topping), lasagne, plaice and scampi. Vegetarian items are available every day, and a special evening menu, giving a good choice of three courses, is served from 6 pm – 10 pm Monday to Saturday.

The beers served from handpumps are McEwans Scotch Bitter, IPA,

Abbot, Pedigree and Theakstons XB. Dry Blackthorn Cider is available on draught, and there is a range of wines and bottled lagers. Opening times are from Monday – Saturday 11 am – 11 pm, Sunday 12 noon – 3 pm and 7 pm – 10.30 pm. Telephone: 081 202 8887.

*How to get there:* The pub is at 3, York Parade, Broadway (the A5) in Hendon, opposite Perryfield Way. Nearest stations: Hendon (BR), Hendon Central (Northern line). Part of the walk is fairly close to Kingsbury (Jubilee line) and Wembley Park (Jubilee and Metropolitan lines). Buses 83 and 182.

*Parking:* No pub car park, but there is a free public car park behind the buildings opposite in Perryfield Way (follow signs).

*Length of the walk:* 5 miles.

*This walk takes you part of the way round the Welsh Harp reservoir, which looks much more natural than many reservoirs, and provides an excellent habitat for waterfowl. The reservoir was established in 1835 as a feeder for the Grand Union Canal, rather than for drinking water, so relatively close access is possible, and it is a popular centre for sailing. 69 acres of the site were designated a Site of Special Scientific Interest in 1950, and this was reaffirmed in 1985. Up to 140 species of birds can be seen here. After leaving the waterside, you go to Kingsbury to see a church that moved, and then walk among some open space in Fryent Country Park. So much green space, and all within sight of Wembley.*

## The Walk
Leave the pub and turn right up Broadway. Cross the Silk Bridge over the Silk Stream feeding the reservoir (the Brent feeds it as well, near Staples Corner). Pass Hendon Court House (1913) on your left, which has a temple-like porch and the Middlesex coat of arms above its entrance. Turn left into Goldsmith Avenue and continue straight ahead onto West Hendon playing fields. Turn left into the car park, and take a flag-stoned path to the left of a pavilion and the tennis courts, and continue to the left of a hedge past the bowling club. To the left there is a reedy area of water and trees.

Keep straight ahead at the end of the hedge, following the water on the left. A path trodden in the grass is discernible, becoming a better defined muddy track. Follow it as it veers to the right, going uphill slightly, emerging onto rough grassland. Follow the path at the edge of this parallel to the bank below. The path enters scrubland with trees, and veers to the left, down to the water. At the water's edge, turn right. The reedy area on the left is a good breeding area for birds and you are asked to avoid it between April and July.

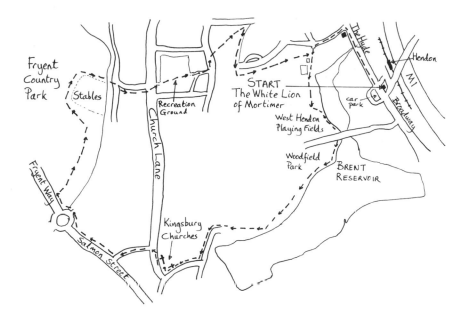

The reeds attract reed warblers, water rails and bitterns. The great crested grebe colony is one of the largest in the country. On the water between here and the rowing centre on the opposite bank you should see many types of waterfowl. Plants growing around the water's edge include flowering rush and yellow flag iris. Follow the path round the bank to Cool Oak Lane.

Cross the lane and take the path opposite following the line of the bank and forking left as it ascends, staying near the bank. The opposite bank has muddy shores that are feeding grounds for tufted duck, pochard, and smew. The Brent reservoir was called the Welsh Harp after a nearby pub which was demolished to make way for the road building schemes which have given us the beauty of Staples Corner, on the opposite bank. The path now passes along the left of a yacht club fence. After this, there is open grassland, then a rifle range on the right. The track becomes a tarmac path; you may see a heron among the trees here. Wembley Stadium becomes visible ahead, and you approach the area of the dam forming the lake. Follow the path behind the sailing club, then take the road from its car park, following it round to the left. Turn left into Old Church Lane (barred to traffic), enter the churchyard on the right and walk through it to pass to the left of the small church ahead.

This is St. Andrew's old church and most of the building is 13th century, although the south door is 12th century, and some of the stonework may be much older. It is preserved by the Wembley Historical Society Trust. This church was too small for the expanding parish in the 19th century, so a new parish church was built on Kingsbury Road. The parish then acquired a third church in 1933, the large one, also St. Andrew's, standing next to St. Andrew's old church. This is a recycled church as it was built between 1845 and 1847 by Dawkes and Hamilton, not here but in Wells Street, Marylebone. Its congregation had shrunk in the 20th century, so this fine example of 19th century Perpendicular style was moved stone by stone and re-erected here. It was reconsecrated in 1934. It is complete with its 19th century furnishings, a remarkable instance of preservation.

Leave the churchyard at the front entrance onto the junction of Church Lane with Old Church Lane and turn right onto Church Lane then left into Queen's Walk to come to Salmon Street. Turn right, go up to the roundabout and straight across it onto Fryent Way. A short distance along on the right is the open space of Fryent Country Park. Take a path to the right behind the houses and follow it uphill. The path breasts a ridge, giving a good view ahead, the open space giving a rural feel to this urban area. The path veers to the left as it skirts a stables and its fields. Turn right at the end of the fence and leave the country park onto Slough Lane, going straight ahead, following the sign to Kingsbury Free Church.

Cross Church Lane and take a path directly opposite leading to Kingsbury Green recreation ground. Go across this (games permitting), heading slightly to the left to exit onto Elthorn way, going straight on to the end of this on Townsend Lane. Cross here to return to West Hendon playing fields. You are now going to walk up the slope to the left for a view over the reservoir and its surrounding open space, but if you're feeling tired, walk straight across the field to the hedge at the border and skip the next paragraph.

Turn left and walk up Townsend Lane at the edge of the parkland until you come to a tarmac path leading across the top to the right. Follow this and enjoy the view to the right. You appreciate what a resource this expanse of water and open space is in such a built-up area. Do not proceed onto Kingsbury Road, but towards the end of the path turn right to come downhill again at the edge of the park, following the hedge and fence.

Continue past the end of Fryent Grove and turn left where the fence does, onto a scrubland area. Walk straight across the edge of this, then go through a gap in the hedge onto mown grassland near playing fields, following the fence and then a line of trees past a play area then tennis courts on the left and the changing rooms on the right. Now walk up to the exit from the car park onto Goldsmith Avenue, turn right at The Hyde, and retrace your steps to the pub.

#  Camden
## The World's End

The World's End is a giant free house in a lively part of Camden, on a site between Camden Road, Greenland Road and Bayham Street. The present imposing building was built about 1875, at least the third pub on the site of the Olde Mother Red Cap, a 17th century alehouse opened when Camden was in rural Middlesex. The pub became popular as a halfway house between the City and Hampstead. Its popularity increased further when public executions began nearby in 1776. Mother Red Cap herself was reputedly the pub's first landlady. She is now a semi-legendary figure in Camden Town, associated with tales of witchcraft, but a more believable story is that she was the widow of a hanged sheep-stealer, selling ale to make a living.

This is a city pub with no garden or facilities for children, and no admission to dogs, but it is a rewarding destination for grown-ups, as it serves a great range of real ales. In the evenings, it is highly popular with a mainly young clientele, but at lunchtimes, the pub attracts a clientele of mixed age and gender. At the pointed end of the cavernous interior is a real ale bar. Towards the back there is a food servery, a basement dining area and then the balcony bar, above which is a balcony seating area. Food is served between 12.30 pm and

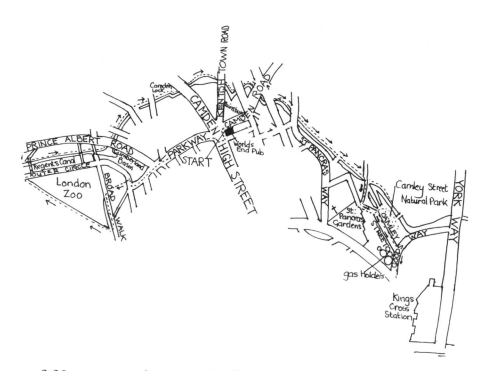

2.30 pm, seven days a week. These are appetising, sustaining meals such as casseroles, chilli, lasagne or cottage pie, served in generous portions with rice or potatoes and two vegetables, or a salad selected from an attractive range. A traditional roast is served on Sundays.

An enormous range (changing regularly) of beers is carried, including Abbot, Wadworth 6X, Theakston, Adnams, King & Barnes, Marston's Pedigree, Ruddles County, Webster's, Tiger, Bateman, Boddingtons, John Smiths, and Courage Best and Directors. Opening times are Monday – Saturday 11 am – 11 pm, Sunday 11 am – 3 pm and 7 pm – 10 pm. Telephone: 071 267 5086.

*How to get there:* The pub is at 174 Camden High Street, at its junction with Camden Road. Nearest station: Camden Town (Northern line) is directly opposite. Buses 168, 24, 29, 253 and 31 stop nearby.

*Parking:* No pub car park, the nearest being the Camden Road Sainsbury's. As this is not a circular walk, it's best to come by public transport.

*Length of the walk:* 3¼ miles.

74

*An easy stroll along flat, paved paths, this walk explores a corner of Regent's Park and then a section of the Regent's Canal towpath. London's canals are ecological corridors from rural to urban environments, so the towpath reveals a rich variety of wildlife. The towpath walk begins by London Zoo, then continues past Camden Lock, becoming more industrial in character, passing old warehouses, and the listed St. Pancras gasholders. Beyond here is the highlight of the walk, Camley Street Natural Park, 2 acres teeming with wildlife, surrounded by industrial wasteland.*

*This is not a circular walk – you start near Camden Town Underground station and finish two stops down on the Northern line at King's Cross.*

## The Walk

Leave the pub, cross Camden High Street, and go straight up on Parkway. At the crossroads continue straight ahead over the bridge, and then walk to Regent's Park via Albany Street and Gloucester Gate, crossing the Outer Circle (the park perimeter road) at Gloucester Gate by the traffic lights, to enter the park.

Regent's Park was laid out by John Nash in 1810-1838, for the Prince Regent, on the site of Marylebone Park used by Henry VIII for hunting. It is bounded by elegant Nash terraces on three sides and by the Regent's canal. In the park, walk straight ahead with the children's playground to your left. At the T junction turn left onto Broad Walk with London Zoo on the right. At the end, before the fountain, turn right onto a short path between bushes, trees and toilets, then turn right at the end, with the zoo again on your right. Beyond, on the left are the dome and minaret of Regent's Park mosque. Continue with the zoo on your right. Leave the park at an exit onto the Outer Circle. Cross the road, and then the canal via the bridge.

Turn left immediately after the bridge, then sharp left at the T junction onto a paved path (the canal is now on your right). Follow this to the towpath and continue in the same direction (the canal still on your right). This section of Regent's Canal, cutting through the zoo, was opened on the Prince Regent's birthday, 12th August 1816.

Further along the canal bends sharply to the left – the intended route through Regent's Park was not allowed, hence the detour round the park. To the right is Cumberland basin, originally a ¾ mile arm (filled in with war rubble in 1948) serving a hay market. You shortly pass a mock castle, the Pirate Youth Club, and then Camden Lock and its famous market. The lock is the first since Cowley near Uxbridge, and the first of 12 between here and Limehouse, a drop of 86 ft. Just before the lock, cross the canal using the oblique bridge and pass the lock-keeper's cottage (1815), converted in 1985/86 into Regent's Canal information centre.

Cross the canal by the roadbridge, keeping to the left to return to the towpath. You pass Camden Lock market which has all mushroomed from a small initiative to utilize some of the then derelict buildings on Dingwalls Wharf in 1972.

Go under the bridge, which, like many, has deep grooves in the ironwork worn by tow ropes. Several tunnels pass under the canal near here. These include the 'Camden Catacombs', formerly used for horses by the railway company, and the Northern line of the Underground – Camden Town has the most complex underground interchange in the system, as the Northern line has two branches going north and south from here. Two Second World War deep air-raid shelters also run from Camden Town station. The ground here must resemble a Swiss cheese.

On the right, after the bridge, is where canal cruises start. Follow the towpath past the lock and under Kentish Town Road Bridge. Opposite is canalside housing (Grand Union Walk) forming part of the 1988 High-tech Sainsbury's complex. Its architect, Nick Grimshaw, also designed Sainsbury's Homebase at Brentford.

After Camden Street Bridge, the canal swings to the right. The river Fleet, a totally enclosed part of the sewer system since 1825, passes under the canal near here. Beyond Camden Road Bridge, on the opposite side is Devonshire Wharf, occupied by Lawfords builders' merchants since the 1860s. No longer supplied by canal, the wharf still gives an idea of how such a site looked during the canal's working life.

Pass under Royal College Street Bridge. To the right is a former piano factory (1904, restored 1986). Continue under St. Pancras Way Bridge, with the Constitution pub prominent next to it. You now pass south of Agar Town, in Victorian times a notorious slum area. Houseboats are usually moored along here. Leave the towpath at the next bridge, Camley Street Bridge, and turn right, crossing the canal.

Before going under the railway bridges, turn right to explore Old St. Pancras church, the oldest building in the borough. Leave the churchyard the way you came in, and go under the bridges to enter Camley Street Natural park. This park was created from industrial wasteland, which itself was carved out of part of the ancient Forest of Middlesex. The park, run by the London Wildlife Trust, is open Saturday – Thursday until 5 pm (closed Fridays). Several different habitats have been created in this small space, and a great variety of plant and animal life is establishing itself here. Sadly, redevelopment at King's Cross threatens this green oasis. The park's Nature Centre has more information (group organisers should telephone in advance on 071 833 2311).

Continue down Camley Street, pass the magnificent Victorian gasholders, turning right onto Goods Way, then go along Pancras Road by St. Pancras station, to finish at King's Cross.

# 18 Monken Hadley
## Ye Olde Monken Holt

This is a charming little pub with a delightful olde worlde interior. It has wooden panelling, a cosy, congenial atmosphere with open fires in cold weather, a collection of old bric-a-brac, such as an old Box Brownie, at the top of the panelling, and a dumb waiter. For animal lovers there is an added bonus of the friendly resident cat and dog, and you can also bring your own dog into the pub. In fine weather, you can sit in a beer garden at the rear of the pub. Children are not allowed in the bar but are welcome in the garden.

Excellent and very reasonably priced hot meals are served from Monday to Saturday (not on Sundays) 12 noon – 2.30 pm, with salads available until 9 pm. There are usually three or four appetizing home-cooked daily specials, accompanied by fresh seasonal vegetables, and very reasonably priced. The desserts, such as fruit crumbles and pies, are also home-made.

This is a Courage house, serving Courage Directors and Best Bitter. Bottled Dry Blackthorn and Autumn Gold Cider are available. Opening times are Monday – Saturday 11 am – 11 pm and standard Sunday hours.

Telephone: 081 449 4280.

*How to get there:* The pub is at 193 High Street, Barnet, part of the Great North Road (A1000). The pub is on the left shortly before Hadley Green. Nearest station: High Barnet (Northern line).

*Parking:* There is no pub car park, but try nearby streets and round the green.

*Length of the walk:* 4 miles (inn GR 245970).

*This varied walk, with no stiles to climb, begins at Hadley Green, where the very fine collection of Georgian houses and peaceful streets now give little clue that it was a place of slaughter – the Battle of Barnet, where the forces of Edward IV defeated those of Henry VI. After passing the Georgian houses and the village church, you walk through Hadley Common and Hadley Wood, and return to the village through King George's Field. This is an excellent route for dog owners and you will meet many local residents out with their dogs on different parts of the walk.*

## The Walk

Leave the pub, cross the High Street, walk left a little way and take Hadley Green Road, the right fork, by the 1885 marble drinking fountain. There are some elegant houses on the right, and on the left is a pond with a variety of wildfowl. A little way beyond Hadley House, an imposing Georgian mansion, is Livingstone Cottage on the right, and a plaque notes that David Livingstone lived there in 1857.

Hadley Green to your left, and the surrounding countryside, was the location of the Battle of Barnet in the Wars of the Roses in 1471, where the Earl of Warwick ('the Kingmaker') was killed, having unwisely changed sides a little before. Edward IV went on to win final victory at the Battle of Tewkesbury, and to enter London and kill Henry VI within weeks of the Battle of Barnet. An obelisk along the Great North Road, where it becomes Hadley Highstone, commemorates the battle.

Follow Hadley Green Road round to the right. You pass more ponds on the left, and then Wilbrahams Almshouses, built 1612, on the right. Keep straight on towards the church, passing another impressive Georgian house behind a gate on the left. Enter the churchyard of St. Mary's church which was founded in the 12th century. The present building dates from 1494 and it was restored in 1848. The flint and ironstone tower has an unusual feature, an 18th century beacon on the top. St. Mary's has a valuable collection of church plate, some of it on loan to the British Museum. Walk straight ahead through the churchyard, passing the church on your left.

On leaving the churchyard turn left onto Camlet Way. Walk just over 150 yards to Monken Hadley C of E primary school, next to

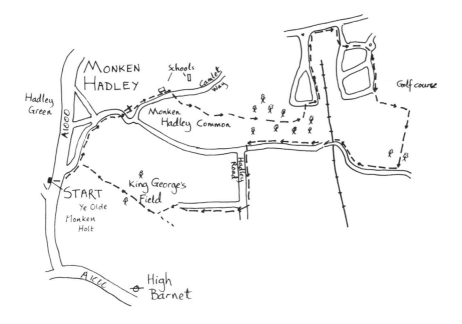

St. Martha's Convent school. Cross the road here and take the grassy path which leads straight ahead over Monken Hadley Common towards the trees. Take the path to the left just before the steep ridge ahead, follow this round to the right, then take the first turning right. Follow the path which veers left downhill through the trees.

You are entering Hadley Wood, which was originally part of ancient Enfield Chase, the royal hunting ground. There is a definite clearing here in the undergrowth, indicating the way, more or less straight ahead. Walk through this clearing and eventually you cross a drainage ditch using a footbridge of two sleepers. Follow the fairly well-defined path straight ahead and cross another footbridge and turn left, keeping the drainage ditch on the left. Keep straight ahead towards the railway line (you can't see it yet, but you will hear the trains) and, when you see the backs of houses on the left, turn left, cross the drainage ditch once more, and walk towards the houses. Take the public footpath straight ahead between the houses and turn right onto Parkgate Crescent. Follow it round onto Parkgate Avenue. Walk to the top of Parkgate Avenue and turn right onto Camlet Way. Walk along here. You are walking over the railway lines you heard earlier, hidden in a tunnel under Great Broadgates Hill, just before Hadley Wood station.

Turn right down Beech Hill Avenue, veer left and then turn right at the T junction. Where the road turns right to become Covert Way, turn left onto a footpath going down the grass bank and cross a footbridge into the wood. Almost immediately after this, take the left fork and you come to the boundary of Hadley Wood golf course. Follow the path to the right and you emerge into an open field. Keep the fence to your left and walk along the field edge. About halfway down the field, there is a well-defined path to the right across the field. Follow this towards the trees on the far side, and continue to follow the path through the wood straight ahead. Keep going until you reach a T junction with a well-defined track. Turn right and follow the track, which becomes a tarmac track (Hadley Wood Road) and then crosses the railway over the brick bridge. This side of the railway, the track is called Bakers Hill, and becomes a proper road. This brings you to the main road and you turn left here where the road narrows for an old gateway, to go downhill on Hadley Road (signposted Hadley Hotel). At Hadley Hotel, turn right onto Tudor Road. Follow this to the end, then take a footpath heading left diagonally across the field. This meets a gravel path at the bottom. Turn right here to follow the path through a gap in the hedge into the next field. Ignore the right fork and follow the now muddy path across this narrow strip between the two fields through the next hedge (which is also a line of trees). Cross a bridge over a stream.

Two paths can now be discerned crossing the field in front of you – take the right hand one, passing to the right of a clump of trees and bushes. This is King George's Field, a very pleasant uncultivated meadow enclosed by trees and shrubs which are a haven for birds. Follow the path uphill, passing through another hedge, then continue across the meadow, the path more or less keeping to the line of the ridge.

You are quite elevated here, and there are good views behind you; take time to look around you. Over to the left is the Church of St. John the Baptist in Barnet. Pass through the gate in the wooden fence at the top and continue to the road ahead. Take the left hand exit from the field, and turn left. You are at the pond where Hadley Green meets the Great North Road. Continue round to the left to return to the pub.

# **Finchley**
# The Five Bells

This Chef & Brewer pub is on a site occupied by a pub for some considerable time. It was rebuilt in 1812, destroyed by fire 50 years later and again rebuilt. The pub is set back from the road by a tree-shaded lawn containing a number of tables and benches – an ideal waiting place for dogs. There is a children's play area at the side.

Inside, there are a couple of older bars and a new conservatory, where children can eat with their parents. Food is served seven days a week, 12 noon-2.30 pm and 6 pm-10 pm. A wide range of hot and cold food is available, including desserts. On weekdays there are two daily specials, and all food is cooked to order at weekends.

Real ales served are Courage Best, Webster's Yorkshire Bitter and Ruddles County. Strongbow Cider is on draught. Bar opening hours are from Monday to Saturday 11 am-3 pm and 5.30 pm (Saturday 6 pm) to 11 pm, Sunday 12 noon-3 pm and 7 pm-10.30 pm.

Telephone: 081 833 1714.

*How to get there:* The pub is between Talbot Avenue and Stanley Road, at 165 East End Road, which runs south westwards off the Great North Road. Nearest Underground station: East Finchley (Northern line).

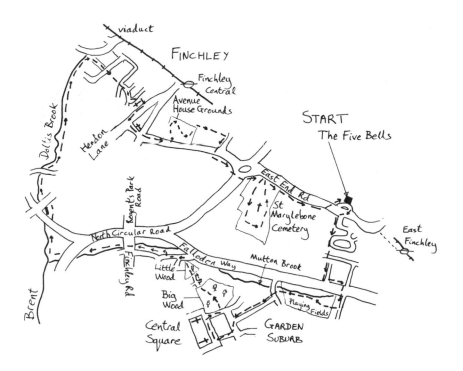

*Parking:* In the pub car park.

*Length of the walk:* 6¾ miles.

*This walk starts off with a stroll through some of Hampstead Garden suburb, then follows part of the Dollis Valley Greenwalk to Finchley, passing a naked lady. No open countryside, but much urban green space, some woods and running water.*

## The Walk
Leave the pub, turning left, and cross East End Road into Cromwell Close, almost opposite. Keep straight on following a footpath between the houses and garages. Emerge into Abbots Gardens and keep straight on down a footpath by number 83 onto Brim Hill. Cross over, turn left and then almost immediately right onto a footpath leading to Cornwood Close. Go down this to Lyttleton Road. Turn left, cross at the central reservation, and enter Norrice Lea, the first turning right. Pass the synagogue, then, after number 16, turn right onto the footpath to Lyttleton playing fields. From the playing fields, there is a fine view of the buildings on Central Square of the Garden Suburb. Turn right and follow the line of trees. Keep to the tarmac path,

passing the bowling green, tennis courts and children's play area. At the end of the hedge, strike out to the right across the grass and turn left at Mutton Brook to follow the tarmac path. Leave the park through the avenue of trees and turn left onto Kingsley Way, then right into Middleway. Walk up the hill through a mixture of brick house types which typify Hampstead Garden Suburb.

Walk up the hill, turn left at Bigwood Road, right onto Southway, and right at the church to enter Central Square, the suburb's one focal point, contrasting markedly with the housing. On the northeast side of the square are the Barnett School and the Hampstead Garden Suburb Institute, for adult education. Pass the Institute, and turn right down Northway. Opposite Bigwood Road, turn left and follow the path into, logically enough, Big Wood, an old broadleaf wood (mainly oak), rich in shrubbery, a haunt for squirrels and birds. Walk through the centre of the wood, following the arrows on green backgrounds to the right at the first T junction and then left almost immediately after. The arrows mark the route of the Dollis Valley Greenwalk (DVG), which runs for 14 miles to Moat Mount at Mill Hill. Follow the arrows across the next crossroads, then leave the wood, following the DVG arrows straight ahead along Denman Drive (South and North), and enter Little Wood. Follow the arrows through the wood past the open air theatre to exit on Addison Way.

Turn left, follow the arrow, go along Addison Way, then just after number 133, take a footpath to the right indicated by a DVG arrow. An overgrown area widens out into parkland with Mutton Brook on your right. Follow the path and DVG arrows and do not re-emerge onto Addison Way. Cross a small footbridge and emerge at the North Circular Road roundabout. To the right, not far down Regent's Park Road, is a bronze statue of a sword-brandishing woman. This is *La Deliverance*, presented to Finchley to mark the Battle of the Marne, but called locally the Naked Lady.

Cross Finchley Road and take the tarmac path opposite. Go under the North Circular Road, and turn right at a T junction, Mutton Brook here joining Dollis Brook (which you now follow on your left) to form the Brent. The trees lining the brook are part of ancient woodland.

Go under the Great North Way, pass a garden centre and then under Hendon Lane, by a weir where the stream drops about 10 ft. Re-emerge into parkland, still following the DVG arrows along a tarmac path leading past much wild habitat. Cross Waverley Grove, go past much shrubby undergrowth, and then across parkland and to the left of a children's play area. After a footbridge, the green area broadens into Windsor Open Space. Follow the DVG arrows. The Open Space narrows and you pass another footbridge on the left, then playing fields on the right. Leave the DVG here by turning right at a T junction to follow a flag-stoned path between the playing fields. Cross Lyndhurst Gardens onto the footpath almost opposite, enter Church Crescent opposite, walk uphill and take a footpath on the right just after a 90° bend in the road. Follow the footpath through the churchyard to St. Mary's parish church.

Emerge onto Hendon Lane. The distinctive brick building to the right with the spire and green copper roof is the old Christ's College building, vacated in 1991. Turn right and go down Hendon Lane onto which the three southwest facing gable ends of the college proclaim the date 1860 and ER, the architect's initials (Edward Roberts). Pass passageways between Nos. 36 and 34 to Park Cottages, where the village firefighters once lived. Nos. 48 and 50 Hendon Lane housed Finchley Fire Brigade's horse-drawn fire engines. Park House, No. 56 (facing Gravel Hill) is one of the few Georgian houses remaining in the vicinity. No. 58, next to the Victorian pillar box, was part of a gate lodge (to Grass Farm) also designed by Edward Roberts.

Now go down Gravel Hill, passing the neo-Byzantine Roman Catholic church of St. Philip the Apostle, and cross over into East End Road. You arrive at Avenue House. Its last private owner, H.C. Stephens (then MP for Finchley), made a number of exotic plantings, and leaflets are available locally describing a route past 87 listed trees.

Enter the parkland via the stable block, then turn left and follow the path round the rear of the house and the perimeter of the park. The path then runs parallel to The Avenue, behind the grounds. Continue straight ahead, ignoring a left fork, then the path veers to the right into the centre of the park. Turn left to pass a walled private area on the right, then turn left onto the path and exit the grounds by turning right onto The Avenue, an ancient track leading to the parish church. Turn right at the end onto Manor View, and then left onto East End Road. Behind the brick wall opposite is the former Finchley Manor House, built in 1723, and now a centre for Judaism.

At the roundabout ahead cross the North Circular Road via the footbridge. Continue along East End Road to the entrance of St. Marylebone cemetery. This is open 9 am-6 pm (Sunday 11 am-6 pm) March-October, closing at 4.30 pm in winter.

Walk down West Avenue, to the right of the chapel. At the top you pass the grave of Keith Blakelock, the policeman killed in the 1985 Broadwater Farm riot. Pass an enormous grey and pink marble sarcophagus, the memorial to an Australian, Thomas Skarratt Hall. At South Avenue, turn left, then return to the entrance on East Avenue. Other prominent people buried here include Austen Chamberlain and the conductor Stokowski. Leave the cemetery the way you came in, then turn right to return to the pub.

# **Finsbury Park**
## 20 The World's End

The World's End is a free house serving a good range of cask-conditioned ales. It opened in 1990, with a large atmospheric interior decorated in Edwardian pub style, featuring cavernous rooms with lots of dark wood panelling, subtly hued gold and purple art nouveau wallpaper, elaborate gold mouldings, wall lights with pretty pink glass shades and brass ceiling fans. It has an ambience resembling a traditional continental café (to the luxurious extent of providing newspapers for the patrons to read). This is very much a town pub, so you should save it for a day when you are not with children or dogs.

Delicious home-cooked food is served at lunchtime six days a week, with a more restricted range on Saturdays (noon – 2 pm Sunday – Friday; filled rolls and pies are available noon – 3 pm Saturday). There is no fixed menu – look on the blackboard for the daily specials. These always include one vegetarian dish which can be more imaginative than is often the case, such as Malaysian peanut curry. An excellent roast lunch is served on Sundays, when live jazz is performed. A variety of live music is played on weekday evenings.

Beers served are Webster's Yorkshire Bitter, Abbot, Wadworth 6X, London Pride and a guest beer, changed every two months. Scrumpy

Jack and Strongbow ciders are available. The opening times are Monday – Thursday 11 am – 11.30 pm, Friday and Saturday 11 am – 12 pm and standard Sunday opening. Telephone: 071 272 8968.

*How to get there:* The pub is just a little north of Finsbury Park Station at 23, Stroud Green Road (A1201). Nearest station: Finsbury Park (Victoria and Piccadilly lines and BR). Bus Nos 29, 253, 259, 279 and W3 stop nearby.

This is not a circular walk. It ends at Alexandra Park and there are frequent buses (W3) and trains from Alexandra Palace (Victoria line, Wood Green and BR, Alexandra Palace) to return to Finsbury Park.

*Parking:* There is no pub car park, but cars can be parked in Finsbury Park (Endymion road entrance). As this is not a circular walk, you could, instead, leave your car in the extensive car parks at Alexandra Palace, and travel to the pub by public transport.

*Length of the walk:* 4¾ miles (to Alexandra Palace).

*After a stroll round Finsbury Park and a brief look at the New River as an introduction, you take the Parkland Walk to Alexandra Palace. This is a disused rail line, now a marvellous corridor for wildlife in the heart of a very built-up area. You also walk through Highgate Wood, and finish in Alexandra Park. You complete the circle by public transport back to Finsbury Park.*

**The Walk**
Leave the pub, turn right on Stroud Green Road and walk down to Seven Sisters Road, going under the railway bridge. Turn left here and almost immediately enter Finsbury Park. Take the road forking right which leads round the park. Then turn left onto a path uphill passing a wooden shelter on the right to the boating lake. Follow the path up and to the left and at the lake turn right. The lake contains a wooded island and acts as host to a variety of waterfowl including Canada geese, greylag geese, tufted duck, scaup, coot, moorhens and mute swans.

Follow the edge of the lake and continue straight ahead past the sports stadium. Then turn left at a shelter and then right following a fence on the right round a horticultural training area. On the left is a sculpture carved from a tree stump. Beyond the sculpture, where the path veers to the right, cut across the grass to the left to join the main path, turn left at the bottom of the path and you will see the New River which is fenced off.

The New River, actually a canal, was built by the rich banker Sir Hugh Myddleton, and was opened on 29th September 1613. It wound from the rivers Chadwell and Amwell near Ware to a reservoir called

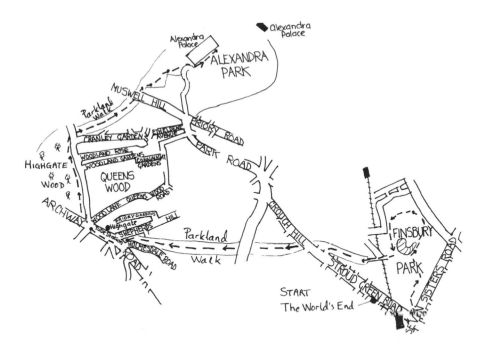

New River Head off Amwell Street in Clerkenwell. From here it distributed water by wooden pipes to various city destinations. Later it was straightened and shortened to terminate at the Stoke Newington reservoirs just east of the park. The river supplied much of North London with water up to 1990.

Follow the main path which veers left, passing on the right the Endymion Road entrance to the park. Soon the western side of the boating lake is reached. Between a café and the end of the sports courts, turn right onto the footbridge over the railway. This becomes an elevated footpath called Parkland Walk, the route of which, along the track of the dismantled Finsbury Park – Alexandra Palace railway, has been preserved from threatened redevelopment and is an unexpected, verdant refuge.

Follow the path straight ahead. At Stroud Green, you pass over a still-working railway line and the former Stroud Green Station building is visible on the right as you walk above Stapleton Hall Road. You pass under a couple of road bridges, and then on the left is Crouch Hill Recreation Centre.

A little beyond here, the platforms of a former station still remain. Further along the path climbs up to the left, as the track of the railway line disappears into a closed-off tunnel under Highgate. Leave the path and turn right onto Holmesdale Road then right onto Archway. Continue up here, crossing over Shepherds Hill and passing Highgate Underground station. Turn right at Muswell Hill Road (by The Woodman), after crossing it. A little way down on the left, enter Highgate Wood by Gypsy Gate.

Highgate Wood was dedicated to the public in 1886, and is maintained by the Corporation of London, not the local Borough. It is a mixed broadleaf woodland, a good habitat for birds, squirrels and joggers. It is open until shortly after dusk. Turn right almost immediately to take a path following the line of the road. Just to your left is a small fenced site enclosed in 1992 to allow natural regeneration to occur. Pass Lodge Gate on the right and the lodge itself on your left. Keep straight on, following the line of the road. Leave the park at the end, turning right to exit by Cranley Gate.

Almost directly opposite is Cranley Gardens. The serial killer Dennis Nilsen killed the last three of his fifteen victims at No 23, having moved there in the vain hope that the inconvenience of disposing of the bodies from an upstairs flat would halt his crimes and it was his own complaint about blocked drains that led to his capture.

Do not cross Muswell Hill Road, but turn left and go down the sloping path to go under the bridge and return to the Parkland Walk. A little way further, a long brick viaduct taking you over St. James's Lane gives you spectacular views to the right. After this, keep straight ahead under the subway and then leave the track of the railway by going up the covered walkway to the right. This takes you into Alexandra Park. Follow the tarmac path, going left at the first fork. You pass through a pleasant leafy area and then into an open park with a café on the left. Strike out half right across the grass. Pass a clump of trees on the left and head in the direction of the TV mast. When you reach the road, walk up to the palace.

Alexandra Palace was built in 1873 as a 'palace for the people', and burned down a month later. It was rebuilt in 1875, and the large hall, with a Willis organ, was used for concerts. The section of the palace with the TV mast on it was the site of the first regular high definition TV service, by the BBC in 1936, the same year that Crystal Palace, the other people's palace, burned down. Alexandra Palace was being restored when it was again almost destroyed by fire in 1980. The burnt-out Great Hall was used as a location (Victory Square) in the film *1984*. It has still not been completely restored, but exhibitions now take place, and there is a bar and restaurant. There is a good view over London from the terrace in front of the palace.

The walk ends here and you can stroll about in the palace gardens or return to Finsbury Park by the frequent public transport.

# **21** **Hendon**
## The Greyhound

The Greyhound at Church End, Hendon is a Richardsons Inn free house, serving food seven days a week. The pub has a number of comfortably furnished bars and is popular with a mixed age-range clientele. There are a few benches outside, and, opposite, a small lawn belonging to the church is available for use by the pub. Children can eat inside with their parents and dogs are no problem.

The extensive menu includes a range of sandwiches and baps, appetizing hot starters/snacks ranging from soup to beefburgers, and more sustaining hot main courses (pie, various types of pasta, giant sausage and ribs) as well as baked potatoes with a choice of toppings. There are a couple of daily specials and a roast at Sunday lunchtimes. Food is served Monday-Saturday 12 noon to 10 pm, and Sundays 12 noon to 2.30 pm, and 7 pm to 10 pm.

Real ales served are Boddingtons Bitter, Abbot Ale, Flowers Original and Castle Eden Ale. Draught Strongbow and lagers and imported bottled premium lagers are also available. Opening hours are Monday to Saturday, 11.30 am to 11 pm, Sundays 12 noon to 3 pm and 7 pm to 10.30 pm.

Telephone: 081 203 1300.

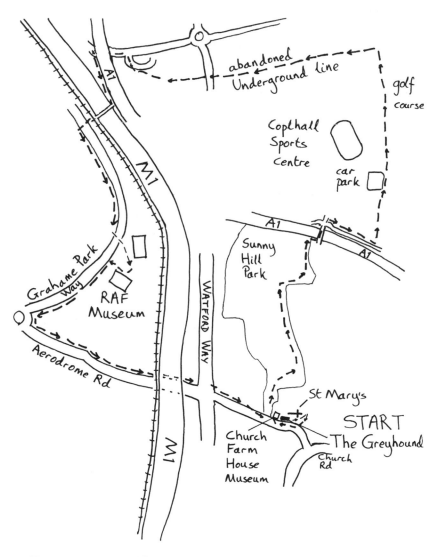

*How to get there:* The inn is at Church End, a continuation of Greyhound Hill, off Watford Way (A41). At its southern end, it leads into Church Road (A504). Nearest Underground stations: Hendon Central and Colindale (both Northern line).

*Parking:* Just a few spaces in front of the pub, but there is a car park at Church Farm House next door.

*Length of the walk:* 4¼ miles (inn GR 228896).

*A pleasant and easy short walk through some of Hendon's older and newer history – over a thousand years of it at the church, a few hundred years of it at Church Farm House Museum and a few decades of it at the RAF Museum. Part of the walk is along a stretch of disused (surface!) Underground line, now a wildlife haven.*

## The Walk

Leaving the pub, turn left and enter the churchyard of Hendon St. Mary's. Enter the church if it is open. The church was founded in 959, a Norman church being built on the site in 1080 – the cubic Norman font in the North aisle, still in use, is said to be the finest example in Middlesex. Sir Stamford Raffles, the founder of Singapore is buried in front of the altar rail. Leave the church and walk round the quiet, almost rural churchyard, then leave it the way you entered, turn right to pass the pub and enter the grounds of Church Farm House Museum.

The museum (admission free) is open Monday-Thursday 10 am-5 pm, Saturday 10 am-1 pm and 2 pm-5.30 pm and Sunday 2 pm-5 pm (closed Friday). Built about 1660, Church Farm House is the oldest surviving house in the parish, and was the centre of a hay and dairy farm for two centuries. The house was used during the Second World War to rehouse bombed-out families and then became derelict. It was renovated and opened as a museum in 1955. The 19th century kitchen and dining room are the centre of an exhibition on life on the farm through the ages. Look round the exhibition, leave the house the way you came in and walk round to the garden at the back, which contains remnants of the farm orchard. Go through the metal gate into the parkland beyond.

Head northward across the parkland directly in front of you, following the avenue of trees to the right of a tarmac path. When you cross a tarmac path at the end of the trees, turn half right and go up the hill to reach the top path. Turn left here to follow the path, admiring the view to your left (to the west). This parkland was part of Church Farm, and is still used for haymaking. Original field boundaries are still marked by trees. Just the other side of the railway and M1 down on the left, you will shortly notice the RAF Museum buildings (marked with RAF roundels). Turn right where the fence on the right does (at a crossroads). To your left (north east), Mill Hill is visible in the distance on the top of the hill and the large green-roofed building is the National Institute for Medical Research. Continue to follow the edge of the parkland, then turn half left downhill following a tarmac path to cut off the corner of the park. Turn left by the fence and follow the edge of the field round to the gateway onto the A1.

Cross the A1 using the footbridge, turn right on leaving the footbridge and walk in front of the houses parallel to the A1, turning left at the sign 'Public Footpath to Mill Hill'. This leads through allotments (round the side of the locked gates). Leave the allotments by the gate at the car park and continue ahead following the line of the fence to your right, crossing the side of the Copthall Sports Centre car park. Leave this by the overlapping wooden fences ahead, and follow the cinder path fenced off on the right from the golf course and on the left from the sports centre. The sides of the path form plenty of wild habitat for insects and birds

Pass through a wooden fence onto a broader tarmac/cinder path, and turn left. There is a blue arrow on the fence indicating the way along part of the disused Mill Hill East to Edgware line of the Underground. This is now heavily overgrown with oak, cracked willow, hawthorn and wild flowers. Nearing Page Street, you approach a disused subway, presumably once the Underground tunnel.

Walk up the ramp on the left of the tunnel to Page Street. Opposite is a footpath between the end of the row of houses and the large Laing complex. Keep straight ahead on this path, turning right at the brick wall, then left into the small estate. Keep straight on into Rowlands Close and follow this round to the right to emerge onto Bunns Lane. Turn left here, go past the garage and then under the A1 road bridge. Immediately afterwards, go up the steps on the left to the level of the A1. Turn right at the top then, just past the garage, cross the M1 via the footbridge and the railway via the subway. Emerge onto Grahame Park Way behind Hendon College and turn left.

You now come to the RAF Museum. Opening hours are 10 am-6 pm daily, last entry 5.30 pm (admission charge). The entire history of the RAF is covered by the aircraft displayed and many, sadly, are the last surviving examples of their type. One hall is devoted to the Battle of Britain display. The museum occupies part of the site of the former RAF Hendon and, as you leave the museum, turning left onto Grahame Park Way, you can see, through the fencing, a derelict part of the former aerodrome. Flying was started here in 1910-1911, when this area was open grassland, by the English aviator Claude Grahame-White, after whom Grahame Park is named.

At the roundabout (Colindale Underground Station is very close along Colindale Avenue, straight ahead), turn left onto Aerodrome Road, and pass the former entrance to RAF Hendon. Pass the Metropolitan Police Training Establishment and go under the railway bridge and the M1. Cross the busy dual carriageway (Watford Way) by the subway to your left. Go up Greyhound Hill, left out of the subway. Pass Church Farm House Museum and return to the pub.

# 22 Harmondsworth
## The Crown

This is a very friendly village pub, which opens long hours and serves food at lunchtimes and evenings seven days a week, thus providing a welcome at most times to hungry and thirsty walkers. There is a small garden and play area at the rear. The pub has several nooks and crannies, with separate rooms for sitting and eating, as well as a no-frills public bar. Brick walls and low timbered ceilings give a cosy atmosphere.

The extensive menu covers snacks (toasted sandwiches are popular with regulars) to full meals of good traditional English food such as steak and kidney pie, all very reasonably priced. There are nearly always vegetarian dishes on the menu. Children are welcome to eat with their parents, preferably in the room behind the bar. Food is served Monday to Saturday 11 am – 2.30 pm and 6 pm – 9.30 pm, Sunday 12 noon – 2 pm and 7 pm – 9 pm.

This is a Courage house, serving Courage Best and Directors Bitter, and Brakspear Bitter (guest beer). Scrumpy Jack Cider is available. The opening times are Monday to Saturday 11 am – 11 pm, and standard Sunday hours.

Telephone: 081 759 1007.

*How to get there:* The Crown is in High Street, off Hatch Lane, which, together with its continuation Holloway Lane, connects the M4 exit 4 to the A4 near the western end of Heathrow Airport. Nearest station: West Drayton (BR).

*Parking:* Some spaces in front of the pub, and around the village green.

*Length of the walk:* 3¼ miles (inn GR 059778).

*Effectively enclosed by the M4, M25 and Heathrow Airport, Harmondsworth has a very rural atmosphere. Its enormous tithe barn is one of the finest in Middlesex. The walk begins in the centre of the village, leaving it by quiet lanes to follow the Wraysbury river to the Colne. A stroll through the village green of West Drayton then follows, then you return to Harmondsworth for a closer look at the tithe barn and parish church. There are good opportunites to see much birdlife. The paths are easy to follow, and there are no hills.*

## The Walk

Leave the pub, turn left and walk past the triangular village green and the church, following Moor Lane to the left. As you leave the village, the tithe barn is visible across the field to the right. Cross the canalised Duke of Northumberland's river (built to supply Syon Park with water) via the humpback bridge, and come to where Moor Lane joins Accommodation Lane (Moor Lane is blocked to traffic here). Keep straight on past Saxon Way, the entrance to an industrial estate, and then the road ends for vehicles, continuing as a public footpath over the river Colne.

The proximity of all this water (there are three rivers here, and reservoirs to the south) attracts birds to the area, particularly gulls. This is a problem for Heathrow Airport, the main runways of which are only a few hundred yards away. The airport carries out a number of measures to discourage birds, some low-technology, like allowing the grass to grow (birds feel unsafe if they can't see predators), and some high-technology, such as broadcasting tape recordings of bird distress calls. All of this psychological warfare moves the birds away from the airport to surrounding areas. Most problems have been caused by starlings, pigeons, crows, lapwings and gulls. At the airport, the gulls have apparently developed the eerie habit of roosting overnight in great numbers in a quiet aircraft parking area by Terminal 3.

Now cross the third of these rivers, the Wraysbury, taking in a footpath to the right to follow the line of the bank. The waterplants, trees and undergrowth by the river provide an excellent mixed habitat. Although this looks wild and untouched you soon come to

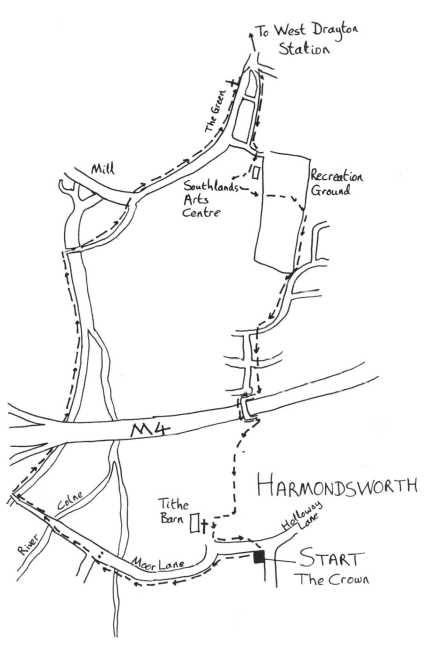

To West Drayton Station

The Green

Mill

Southlands Arts Centre

Recreation Ground

M4

Colne

River

Tithe Barn

HARMONDSWORTH

Holloway Lane

Moor Lane

START
The Crown

signs of human presence as you pass under the series of bridges carrying the M4 to the intersection with the M25. Emerge onto a riverside road. The scenery on the left is a bit of an industrial wasteland along here, but the river is attractive enough, with its trees and islands, and you should see plenty of waterfowl. You pass some large ponds surrounded by trees where you may see a heron. Cross the river by turning right (signposted 'Public Byway') over the Bailey bridge.

You are now on Cricketfield Road. Walk past the cricket field to come to Mill Road. Before passing the Angler's Retreat on the right, you can see an old brick bridge on the left. Behind this is the derelict mill that named Mill Road, and a mill stream millrace and wheel are still visible if you make a detour to them. Otherwise, turn right at Mill Road and walk into West Drayton passing some impressive houses on the right. You come to The Green, which has a number of good houses facing onto it. Opposite the Catholic church on the left is the former Britannia Brewery, 1806, now redeveloped into housing. Next to the entrance to this is a Regency house. Walk round The Green in a circle, and leave it by Avenue Close, going towards Southlands Arts Centre.

The house dates from the early 18th century, and is open to the public in its role as an Arts Centre. The grounds are open to the public. On the left of the house is a herb garden, then behind the house and to the right of it is a formal garden containing sculptures. Next to the car park is a pond, and beyond this and the barn is an open field, said to be the best place in the area to see wild flowers. A metal kissing gate in the brick wall bounding the field opens onto the adjacent recreation ground. Walk across this until you come to a tarmac path and turn half right onto it.

At the end of the recreation ground, turn half right and follow the path in front of the school, passing the Cat and Fiddle on the left. Turn right onto Rowan Road, follow it round, then turn left onto a path leading to the motorway. Cross the M4 by the footbridge. From the bridge you get a good view of the tithe barn and church. There was once a Benedictine priory in the vicinity of the church and barn. Follow the path across the field towards the church. The path leads into the churchyard. You can get a close view of the tithe barn from the churchyard wall. The barn dates from 1427, when the manor was owned by Winchester College. It is nearly 200 ft long and has wagon doors on the east side.

St. Mary's church is a mixture of many periods from the 12th century onwards. The 12th century south doorway is described by Pevsner as one of the most elaborate pieces of Norman decoration in the country. In the churchyard is buried Richard Cox, a local fruit-grower who developed the Orange Pippin in the mid 19th century. Leave the churchyard by the main gates and return to the pub.

#  Staines
## The Angel Hotel

The Angel Hotel is a former coaching inn dating from 1309, although there is said to have been an inn here from 1085. The High Street was a Roman road so perhaps travellers have had refreshment here for a very long time. The Angel is still a hotel, with 13 rooms available. The interior has plenty of brick and wooden beams in evidence, and in the restaurant part, alcoves are divided by wooden pillories.

Good home-cooked food is served seven days a week, providing an extensive range of home-cooked hot main dishes, including at least one vegetarian course. Bar snacks are available Monday to Saturday 11.45 am-8.30 pm (no food 3 pm-5.30 pm, and the selection diminishes as the day proceeds), and a roast lunch is served on Sundays. The excellent soups are also home-made ('not a thing is wasted in cooking'), as are the desserts, the bread and butter pudding being particularly good. Weekday lunchtimes can get quite busy.

Beers served are Courage Best, Wadworth 6X and Adnams, and Dry Blackthorn Cider is available on draught. Opening times are Monday to Saturday 11 am-11 pm and standard Sunday hours.

Telephone: 0784 452156.

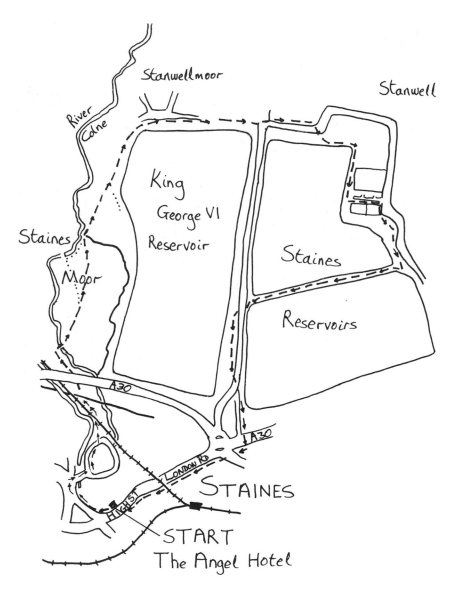

*How to get there:* The hotel is at 24 High Street (the A308), on the right approaching the river (before the town hall). Nearest station: Staines.

*Parking:* Restricted amount available at the pub, but there is a car park at Ashby Recreation Ground on Wraysbury Road (B376), and you may find on-street parking near the former railway station on Moor Lane.

*Length of the walk:* 5¼ miles (inn GR 035716).

*Starting from the centre of Staines, you pass the Town Hall and a former Georgian railway station building (for a Victorian railway) before coming to Staines Moor, a marvellous stretch of common land unploughed for over 1,000 years. The giant reservoir embankments dominate the scene, and after circling the King George VI reservoir you walk back on an elevated path between the two Staines reservoirs, giving you a rare glimpse of the water surfaces. There are a couple of stiles to climb.*

## The Walk

Leave the pub and turn right. On the left, opposite, is the imposing Town Hall. Turn right into Church Street. Cross the river Colne and come to the crossroads with Wraysbury Road. Ahead you can see the tower of the former brewery, now the Maltings development. Turn right onto Wraysbury Road and walk just past Hale Road, the entrance to the industrial estate. At the start of Moor Lane is a brick Georgian building, now offices. This was the former Staines West station, originally a house, then converted by the GWR into a station building in 1880 (to save money). The Staines-West Drayton Line was closed in 1965 by BR (to save more money). Behind the building is evidence of its former function – traces of tracks and platform lighting. Now return to the front of the building, cross the Wraysbury River by the bridge to enter the industrial estate, and turn left. Follow the road round to the right, then take a footpath on the left continuing straight on by the Wraysbury river, signposted public footpath to Stanwellmoor.

Turn right at a stile and cross the railway line (with care) – this is the line to Windsor and Eton Riverside. Follow the path on the other side, turning left, and cross a stile. Follow a yellow arrow on the stile, and cross over the Staines reservoir aqueduct via the brick bridge, then cross the field diagonally to the left heading towards the bridge under the main A30. Go through a kissing gate, then under the bridge, and then through another kissing gate onto Staines Moor.

Staines Moor is ancient common land (since 1065). The freehold belongs to the Lordship of the Manor of Staines, but registered commoners have grazing rights. The moor is a valuable site for wildlife, and was designated one of the first SSSIs in the country in 1955.

Head out across the common aiming just to the right of the first pylon, and then follow the bank of the Colne. Of the many types of plants growing in the meadow, you may see brown sedge, marsh stitchwort and some which are now rare in Britain. Apparently 130 species of birds have been recorded here in recent years. Golden plover winter here in large flocks.

Cross the Colne via the concrete footbridge and follow a yellow arrow directly across the common. The path here is indistinct, but you should be heading in a line towards the edge of the reservoir embankment so that you eventually cross the Bonehead ditch by a wooden footbridge. If you come to a concrete footbridge across the Colne, do not cross it or follow the yellow arrows, but turn right and follow the bank until you come to the Bonehead.

Cross the ditch by the plank bridge, and follow the path skirting the reservoir embankment, then go through a kissing gate onto a concrete path at the foot of the embankment. You pass a gravel workings on the left, and then come to houses at the edge of Stanwellmoor, as the path rounds the corner of the reservoir. After crossing a concrete bridge over a stream, turn right onto a gravel path through the trees, cross a wooden footbridge and then emerge onto the road. Continue to follow the line of the reservoir embankment, then take a path leading past a small brick building on the right and stables on the left.

The path comes out onto Stanwell Moor Road. Cross this at the traffic lights and go into Park Road directly opposite leading to Stanwell. Shortly after, where the road veers sharply to the left, keep straight ahead on a path following the reservoir embankment. This turns sharp right at the corner of the reservoir and runs past a recreation ground – you may find it easier to walk inside the railings of the recreation ground, as the path is overgrown here, and there are openings at the end of the ground to re-enter the path. A short distance further on, the footpath turns left to run to the road along the cemetery and allotments. If it is too overgrown, you may pefer to reach Town Lane by walking along a tarmac path to Lauser Road in the housing estate, going along this past the end of Jubilee Close, then turning right at the T junction (Town Lane). Follow the road alongside the reservoir then turn right onto a footpath (signposted Staines) leading up the embankment. Go through a metal kissing gate and follow the fenced path.

It is not often that you have a vantage point high enough to see the reservoirs, and this path now leads you straight between the two Staines reservoirs, giving you the unusual experience of looking down on two large bodies of water on either side of you. All too soon the path leads down to Stanwell Moor Road, which you need to cross, as the footpath is on the other side. Turn left and walk towards Staines. Cross back again as the road reaches the end of the reservoirs and bends to the right, while you keep straight on, down Stanwell New Road. Come to the main A30. Cross this, turn right, pass the end of Shortwood Common on the left, then cross the Staines bypass at the large roundabout, continuing straight on down London Road. Keep on down this as it becomes High Street and leads you back to the pub.

# 24 Horsenden Hill
## The Black Horse

The Black Horse on Oldfield Lane North in Greenford is right next to the towpath of the Grand Union Canal, and it was apparently built about 200 years ago to house the navvies digging the canal between here and West Drayton. It is now a Fuller's house with an extremely pleasant garden (ideal for parking dogs) by the towpath, and a play area. Children may well prefer to stay here, although they are able to eat indoors. Inside there is a friendly welcoming atmosphere. And a parrot.

Simple but satisfying bar meals are served Monday to Friday lunchtimes until 2.30 pm. There are items such as burgers and chips, sausages, pies, salads and rolls, the latter also being available on Saturdays. No food is served on Sundays, and eating your own sandwiches in the garden is 'tolerated' then – but please ask first.

Beers served are Fuller's London Pride, Chiswick Bitter, and ESB. Strongbow Cider and Heineken are also on draught, and bottled imported lagers are available. The pub is open from 11 am – 11 pm, Monday to Saturday, with the usual Sunday hours.

Telephone: 081 578 1384.

*How to get there:* The Black Horse is at 425 Oldfield Lane North, which leads off the A40 in Greenford, running parallel to the Greenford Road, and passing Greenford Station. The pub is on the left, just before the canal bridge. Nearest station: Greenford (Central line and BR).

*Parking:* In the large pub car park.

*Length of the walk:* 3 ¼ miles (inn GR 149845).

*After a stroll along the towpath of this rural-seeming part of the Paddington arm of the Grand Union Canal, you climb up Horsenden Hill, an area of outstanding natural beauty. Some of the surroundings are preserved as public open space from all the encroaching industry, and you get a good view from the top, which is a popular place for flying kites. You return through meadows and open space to the pub. The walk is not that long, but Horsenden Hill at 275 ft is the highest point in Ealing.*

**The Walk**
Leave the pub, go onto the towpath and turn right to walk under the bridge. Pass a giant bakery on the right, and then go under Greenford Road Bridge. Keep on the towpath, passing natural grassland on the right and pass a footbridge. Be prepared for some mud as the quality of the towpath deteriorates beyond here.

The Paddington arm of the Grand Junction Canal, from Bull's Bridge to the Paddington basin, was planned as a useful extension to the city of the main Grand Junction Canal from the Thames at Brentford to the Midlands and further north. An Act of Parliament for its construction was passed in 1794, and the Paddington arm was completed in July 1801. This terrain is ideal for canals and there is not a single lock on the Paddington arm. The Regent's Canal was built later by a separate company to link Paddington Basin to the Thames at Limehouse and opened in August 1820. The two separate canal companies merged in 1929 to become the Grand Union Canal Company, so all of their combined waterway is now known as the Grand Union Canal. Despite the original industrial purpose of the canal, the scenery on either side of the towpath is very rural and tranquil. Horsenden Hill itself can be seen ahead to the left. The canal and its surrounds are much frequented by waterfowl. On one of our visits here a swan protecting its cygnets effectively blocked the towpath for half an hour before taking to the water with them.

On the right you pass Perivale Wood, another sanctuary for birdlife. After the wood you pass a small green open space and then go under Horsenden Lane Bridge. Leave the towpath immediately after the bridge by going up to the right and cross the canal on the separate

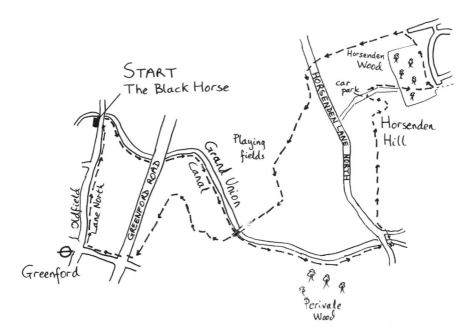

footbridge. Pass the entrance to Horsenden Farm, and then shortly after, the path leaves the roadside and you pass a Horsenden Hill information board.

The Horsenden Hill open space includes relatively recently established woodland, ancient woodland and ancient meadows and hedgerows, the types of wild plants found in them indicating their antiquity. Take the centre path (rough gravel) from the board leading into the trees, not the tarmac path to the left following the line of the road. Pass an area where some now rare wild flowers grow, including cornflower, poppies, corn cockle and camomile, and then enter the wood on an uphill path. Local residents say that foxes are frequently to be seen here. You may not spot any, but you will see that this is a superb piece of wild habitat. Birds are much in evidence. Where the path forks, take the steeper right fork and allow time to admire the view of London.

Veer left by a post with an arrow pointing back the way you have come, following the established yellow gravel path. Pass a guide post (numbered 4) also pointing back the way you have come. Now walk across the flat grassed top of an underground reservoir (passing reverse arrow 3). Just after the end of the reservoir is a broader track, continuing a concrete road. Follow this directly uphill to the flat top of another underground reservoir.

Over to the right is a concrete OS triangulation pillar – the top. Beyond this is the golf course. When you wish to leave the top, continue across the reservoir to another post and arrow pointing back the way you came and take a path curving round to the left. Pass another backwards-pointing arrow and come down into the car park. Arrow No. 1 is in the car park. Turn right, and walk through the car park to enter Horsenden Wood through the overlapping fences.

This is ancient woodland with oak, hornbeam and wild service trees (the wild service is now rare and has leaves resembling maple). Follow the tarmac path through the wood, passing another backwards-pointing arrow. As you start to come out of the wood, do not leave it to go past the houses, but turn left onto a rougher track heading back into the wood. Follow the track to the end of the path, and come to the end of Whitton Drive. Take the first tarmac path to the left (continuing straight on from the road) and follow it to its end on Horsenden Lane North.

Cross the road at the Ballot Box pub, enter a car park for a recreation area, then immediately turn left into the Horsenden Hill Open Space area (open fields) to the left of the pavilion. Take the path along the edge of the field more or less following the line of the road, pass a post with a reverse arrow (17), come to a rough vehicle track and turn right. Take the first path shortly after to the left through the hedge, then take the path to the right following the hedge downhill.

Pass reverse arrow 15, enter a rugby field through the opening in the hedge and turn right to follow the edge of the field. Follow the path round to the left, then turn right at the bottom of the field, go through the opening in the hedge, and turn left to cross the canal by the footbridge.

Take the path meandering through the open space on this side of the canal – you passed by this on the towpath at the beginning of the walk. Most maps still describe this as a golf course, but this is not a particularly fiendish rough area, but public open space, a good mixed habitat of wet areas, grasses, trees and shrubs. Follow the obvious tarmac and gravel path through this and then along the line of Greenford Road, eventually exiting at the open space by the crossroads. Cross Greenford Road and turn right into Rockware Avenue. By the station, turn right into Oldfield Lane and return to the pub.

# 25 Perivale
## The Fox and Goose

This friendly Fuller's pub just off the Hanger Lane gyratory system has been recently refurbished to give a welcoming exterior and outside terrace. The interior is cosy, with a smallish public bar, and a larger carpeted lounge with wood panelling, tables and comfortable seats, and an area at the rear where children are allowed. The garden is a special attraction in hot weather, having a proper lawn, and a well-planted border with shrubs and roses to screen off the view of the car park. Dogs 'under control' can join their owners in both the garden and pub.

Beers served from hand pumps are Fuller's London Pride, Chiswick Bitter and ESB. Two ciders are available on draught, Strongbow and Symond's Scrumpy Jack, as is Grolsch Lager. The Fox and Goose keeps enough wines to warrant having a wine list. The pub is open from 11 am to 11 pm Monday to Saturday, and the usual Sunday hours.

The Fox and Goose is justly proud of its excellent food, and the fact that nearly all of it is home-cooked. On Monday to Saturday, food is served from 12 noon to 9 pm. A full range of hot and cold meals and snacks is available until 3.30 pm. Chicken in various delicious guises is available every day, as is a vegetarian main course and tempting hot

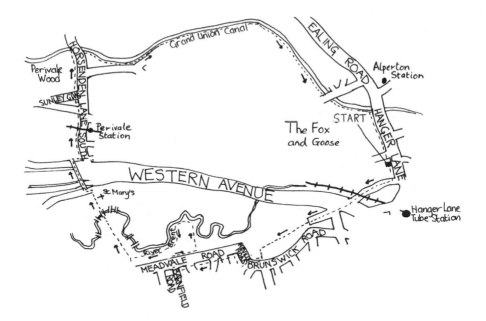

and cold desserts (including traditional favourites such as spotted dick and treacle sponge). After 3.30 pm a more restricted range of items is available but you can still tuck in to such things as steak sandwiches and steaks and burgers cooked to order. On Sundays, a roast meal is served from 12 noon till 2 pm (no food on Sunday evenings).

In the summer, a special feature is the occasional all-day barbecue in the garden, when charcoal-grilled steaks, burgers and sausages (and garlic bread) are available from 12 noon till 9 pm (weather permitting). These are most likely to be held on Saturdays or bank holidays – telephone for information.

Telephone: 081 998 5864.

*How to get there:* The pub is on Hanger Lane (A4005), near the gyratory system (A40 intersection), on the left heading north. Nearest Underground stations: Hanger Lane (Central line) and Alperton (Piccadilly line). The 83 bus (Golders Green/Ealing) passes directly outside the pub (and both stations).

*Parking:* Customers are very welcome to leave their cars in the pub's ample car park.

*Length of the walk:* 4½ miles.

*Perivale which means 'pure valley' or possibly 'pear tree valley' can by no stretch of the imagination be described as picturesque but this easy walk (no stiles or steep slopes) goes through some peaceful rural pockets, in the midst of industrial wasteland and characterless suburbia bisected by the Western Avenue (A40) which was built in the 1920s and is one of London's busiest roads. During the first half of the walk there are glimpses of the meandering river Brent which has its source in Hertfordshire and enters the Grand Union Canal at Brentford. The second half of the walk goes near Perivale Wood, a nature reserve, and then along part of the Grand Union Canal towpath. The canal at this point is rural, skirting first Horsenden Hill and then Sudbury Golf Course both on the opposite side of the canal to the towpath.*

## The Walk

Turn right on leaving the pub and walk along Hanger Lane. Turn right onto Westgate and follow the road round to the left, going under the LT railway bridge and turning right at the A40. Cross this using the subway about 20 yards to the right. At the other side, leave the subway via the steps, turn left into Lynwood Road, then immediately right onto a driveway leading to garages. Continue past bollards straight ahead along the pathway, which has allotments on the right. Walk to the end of the path and turn left onto a paved path. At the end, turn right onto Brunswick Road, right again into Neville Road and then left onto Meadvale Road. These are pleasant tree-lined streets. Walk along here passing Brentham Sports Club. Opposite Barnfield Road turn right into Pitshanger Park.

Follow the path round to the right. As you continue round the edge of the park, the path meets and then skirts the river Brent keeping it on the right hand side. The park is mowed, but the river bank is left wild, which provides a good habitat. At the crossroads where the bowling green begins, turn right along the fenced path between two sections of the Ealing golf course. Cross the bridge over the river Brent, and follow the path straight ahead.

On the right is the church of St. Mary, built in 1135. The present building dates mainly from the 13th century, and the weather-boarded west tower was added in 1510. The church became redundant in 1972 and no regular services are held there, but there are still occasional services such as Harvest Festival. A notice states that it is no longer possible to hold baptismal, wedding or funeral services here, so don't get carried away by the sheer romanticism of the place. There is quite an attractive little churchyard, and inside there are memorials to the Mylett family, who owned a farm where the Mylett Arms is now. From 1976 the church has been an arts centre. Special events include concerts, plays, flower festivals, school art exhibitions and music festivals. The building is open on Sunday afternoons from mid-March to October.

Leave the path via the lychgate, passing to the left of the Mylett Arms, and cross the footbridge over the A40. From here there is a good view of the former Hoover factory which was built in 1932-1935 by Wallis, Gilbert & Partners (who also designed the former Firestone building on the A4, see Walk 9). This Grade II listed building, now called the Hoover Building, is owned by Tesco, who have been refurbishing it (at time of writing) and preserving the impressive art deco façade.

At the other side turn left onto Horsenden Lane South, pass by Perivale station on the right, and continue under the railway bridge and along the road. Hidden from you by buildings, over to the left is Perivale Wood. The 27 acres of woodland, which were once part of the ancient Middlesex forest, consist mostly of oak and hazel trees and are the breeding habitat for at least 70 species of birds. The wood was established as a nature reserve and memorial to Gilbert White between 1902 and 1904, and is administered by the Selbourne Society. It is not normally open to the public, but enquiries about visits can be made by telephoning 081 578 3181.

Continue along Horsenden Lane South to reach the canal towpath, and turn right onto it. On the left is Horsenden Hill, an area of outstanding natural beauty, and a golf course follows on the left. All the way along here the canal and the banks provide a good habitat for birds and insects. The canal turns a bend, and you pass a mooring area. Go under the Bilton Road bridge, the towpath now becoming a good tarmac path. Pass a builders' merchants on the left (many were situated by the canal for ease of transport) and then a Sainsbury's on the right (many of these seem to be situated by the canal, but the reason for this is unclear). A little further on you pass The Pleasure Boat pub on the left, and you leave the towpath here. Alperton underground station is very near. To return to the Fox and Goose, turn right onto Ealing Road and follow it as it becomes Hanger Lane and crosses the river Brent. The pub is on the right.

# 26 Mill Hill
## The Rising Sun

This is one of the oldest inns in the neighbourhood, and was once a stopping place for cattle drovers after the long climb up Highwood Hill. The inn, in Marsh Lane, dates from the 13th century, and the centre is at least 100 years older than the nearby Highwood House (1780). In 1754 it was recorded as being called The Sun, and became The Rising Sun later in the 18th century. There is a garden behind the pub, where barbecues are occasionally held in the summer, and inside there is a central bar with bars off to the sides.

Bar meals are served Tuesday to Saturday 12 noon – 2.30 pm and 7.30 pm – 9 pm, Sunday 12 noon – 2 pm and Monday 12 noon – 2.30 pm. The choice includes an extensive range of pub snacks with daily specials, and sustaining Sunday lunches. Children may eat in the side bars, or, of course, in the garden.

Beers served in this Taylor Walker house are Tetleys Bitter and Burton Ale, plus one guest beer. Opening times are Monday – Friday 12 noon – 3 pm, 5.30 pm – 11 pm and Saturday 11 am – 3 pm, 6 pm – 11 pm, with the usual Sunday hours.

Telephone: 081 959 3755.

109

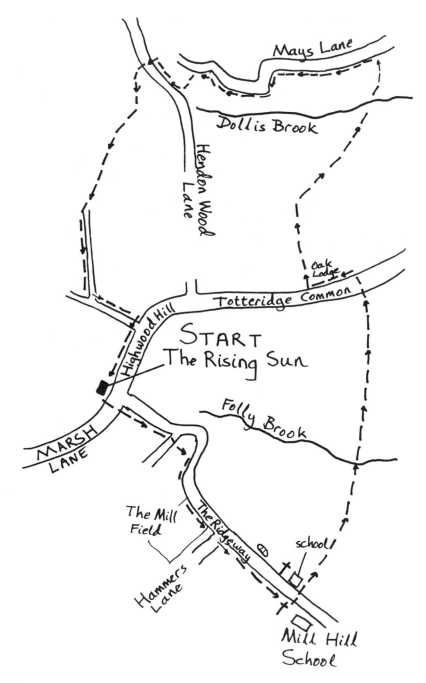

*How to get there:* The pub is at the far end (No. 137) of Marsh Lane (A5109) from its junction with the Watford bypass near the M1, just at the junction with Highwood Hill. Nearest stations: Mill Hill East (Northern line) and Mill Hill Broadway (BR). Bus 240 from Golders Green passes Mill Hill East and along The Ridgeway, turning down Hammers Lane which is on the route of the walk. No. 251 (Monday to Saturday) runs from Arnos Grove to Stanmore, passing along Highwood Hill in front of the pub.

*Parking:* In the pub car park (in side roads when it is busy).

*Length of the walk:* 4 miles (inn GR 218935).

*This is a very pleasant rural walk, with just a few stiles, through open countryside only minutes away from highly built-up areas of London. The walk goes near Mill Hill School, the famous public school, before going across the Folly Brook valley. You return via part of the Dollis Valley walk to Moat Mount Open Space, passing the former homes of two great 19th century figures, Raffles and Wilberforce.*

## The Walk

Leave the pub and walk down Highwood Hill as far as Lawrence Street on the right. Almost directly in front of you is a footpath leading up to the right of 'The Old Forge'. Follow this, then rejoin the road and pass St. Mary's Abbey, and then, on the right, Holcombe House. This was built in 1775 for Sir John Anderson, a Lord Mayor of London. There is restricted admission to the ground floor rooms of the house (2 pm – 4 pm Spring bank holiday weekend, and the last two weeks in August and first two weeks in September).

Just past The Missionary Institute building, on the opposite side of the road, is Belmont School, built in 1765, as a private house for a former Lord Mayor of London, and now a preparatory school for Mill Hill. Opposite this, turn right into Mill Field for the view, then immediately turn left and follow the path parallel to the road. As well as the superb view to the south, there is a fine oak tree to admire. Leave the field at the end to rejoin the footpath, cross Hammers Lane and pass the war memorial. Opposite is a small pond asking you not to cast your bread upon the waters, as uneaten bread is poisoning it. Near this is St. Paul's church, built 1833-36 by William Wilberforce, the source of a dispute with the pro-slavery Rector of Hendon (the local parish), who was hostile to Wilberforce and his friend Raffles. Beyond this on the right are the buildings of Mill Hill School, founded in 1807 as a Nonconformist school, with the buildings dating from 1825. Do not go past the school, but cross The Ridgeway, and take a path almost opposite the school chapel passing between the primary school and the cottages.

This is a pebble path between a fence and a hedge. Climb over a pair of stiles, and keep straight ahead as the path now goes through real working farmland, making you think that you are deep in the country. You get good views as the land dips and rises. Follow the blue arrows to keep on the path as it crosses field entrances. There is a hedge and a line of trees on the right, and a field to the left. The path becomes a dirt track, then you leave the fields via a stile, and come to Totteridge Common, opposite St. Edward's College for Missionaries of Africa. This area of London seems to be Piccadilly Circus for missionaries.

Cross over to the college, turn left, walk past Oak Lodge, then turn right onto a public footpath to Mays Lane by the side of a brick wall through a gate labelled 'Northernhay Cottages'. The path becomes a visible track across a meadow. Cross a stile and a sleeper bridge across a ditch then continue straight ahead, passing a cricket pitch behind a hedge on the left. Go through a wooden kissing gate, following the arrow on it. Come to a fork in the path – take the left fork over a sleeper bridge (Dollis Brook) then over a stile following a yellow arrow. Walk directly across the field to another stile, and leave the field by the stile onto Mays Lane. Turn left, pass The Elizabethans' Sports Ground, and then after a sharp bend in the road to the left, turn left onto a footpath between the houses (with the sign No Cycling, No Horse Riding). Turn right onto Hendon Wood Lane. Walk along here, passing, but not taking, a path signposted as part of the Dollis Valley Greenwalk, then between the houses Green Ridge and Cedar Cottage, cross over onto a dirt path leading via a wooden bridge over a ditch and into the wood beyond. Turn left at a T junction, then turn right at another T junction signposted 'public footpath Mill Hill Moat Mount OS'. Turn left (to the south) at a junction following the arrow on a gatepost, and continue following signs to Mill Hill and Moat Mount Open Space, and the green arrows, straight on until you come to a path to the right signposted public footpath to Stirling Corner.

Do not follow this, but cross a stile onto an unmetalled track and turn left onto the track, signposted to Mill Hill. Cross a stile onto a metalled road. On the left you are passing Wilberforce Woods, the site of Hendon Park, where William Wilberforce lived 1826-1831. His friend and neighbour Sir Stamford Raffles helped him to lay out the estate. On the right, in a white house, Lord Gardiner, a Labour Lord Chancellor, lived until his death in 1990. Pass ponds here on which you may see some exotic swans, the owners of the property using the ponds as a swans' refuge. The road leads onto Highwood Hill. Just to the left is a plaque noting Wilberforce's residence. Turn right, and a little way along, you pass Highwood House, where Sir Stamford Raffles lived. His estate included the Rising Sun, to which you return just past the entrance to Highwood House.

# Totteridge
## The Orange Tree

27

The Orange Tree has a picturesque site set back from the road behind a pond fringed with trees. Benches and tables outside face the pond, and dogs, not allowed in the pub, seem very happy to wait here and watch the world go by. The present building dates from the late 1800s. Before then there were two neighbouring pubs, the other being the Three Horseshoes. They combined under that name, and the pub later became known as the Orange Tree. There has apparently been a pub on the site since the 17th century.

Inside, there is a comfortable lounge bar and a separate Carvery Restaurant. Good pub food, such as two hot daily specials, jacket potatoes and a range of sandwiches (incuding very substantial club sandwiches with chips), is available daily in the bar from 12 noon-2.30 pm, and sandwiches can be obtained all day. The Carvery is open from 12 noon-2 pm and 6 pm-11 pm, and offers complete meals. A range of hot and cold starters can be followed by main courses such as salads, steaks and roast meats, as well as fish and chips, steak pie and two hot vegetarian dishes. A standard dessert is included in the main course price, but sweet tooths can pay extra for a speciality dessert. A nice touch is that two menus are available for children: 12 and under and 7 and under.

The beers served are Charrington IPA, Worthington Best Bitter, and Fuller's London Pride from handpumps, Stones Best Bitter and Strongbow Cider being also on draught. A wine list is available.

Opening times are Mondays to Saturday 11 am-11 pm and standard Sunday hours. Telephone: 081 445 6542.

*How to get there:* Totteridge Village (road) is the A5109, leaving the A1000 at Whetstone and the pub is No. 7, just beyond Totteridge Green, past the school, on the left. Nearest station: Totteridge and Whetstone (Northern line). Part of the walk passes close to the station. Bus 251 (Monday-Saturday) Arnos Grove-Stanmore passes the pub.

*Parking:* On the pub approach drive (this can get busy).

*Length of the walk:* 5½ miles (inn GR 248939).

*Starting with the historic St. Andrew's Church in Totteridge, the walk takes you through some very rural scenery between Mill Hill and Totteridge. You then walk along a section of the Dollis Valley Greenwalk, passing open grassland and managed parkland, before returning to the pub through peaceful Totteridge Green. Totteridge is especially favoured, as parts of it seem to be deep in the country, yet the Northern line to the City is close at hand.*

**The Walk**

Leave the pub, turn left and then left at Totteridge Village (the road). Just to the north are Northcliffe Drive and Harmsworth Way, marking the village's connection with the millionaire family. At St. Andrew's church, cross over to enter the grounds for a closer look. The great yew tree by the church is over 1,000 years old. Yew trees are associated with churches, so a place of worship may have been here that long. The earliest record of a church here is an order of Pope Nicholas IV dated 1291. The church will probably be open.

Leave the churchyard by the lychgate, cross the road, and go down a footpath opposite the church porch between Nos. 41 and 43, marked by a yellow arrow and signposted Mill Hill. After a short while, the houses on the right give way to open countryside. The hedge on the right and the trees on the left almost form a canopy over the path, making it resemble a tunnel through greenery.

To the left is a wildlife reserve centred round Darlands Lake, where there are occasional Open Days, but otherwise no public access. You can see some of the broadleaf wood surrounding the lake from the path. On the right, high up on the ridge, you can see the backs of some of the exclusive houses on Totteridge Common. At the end of the

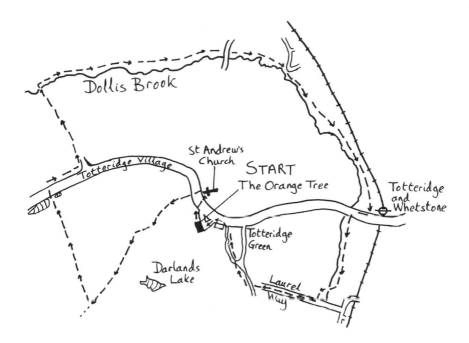

enclosed path is a stile. Cross this following the yellow arrow and walk across the centre of the field, following the path heading towards the large green-roofed building on the horizon (the National Institute for Medical Research in Mill Hill).

Cross the stile at the edge of the field. Folly Brook is on the left, and immediately next to this turn right onto a path signposted Long Ponds, Totteridge, and also marked by red and yellow arrows. This path is fenced off from the field, with a hedge on the right, with mostly gravel underfoot. The path climbs, so turn round for the view every now and then.

Cross a stile at the end of the path, pass the end of the Long Ponds, and cross Totteridge Common (the road). Turn right, following the yellow and red arrows. Pass Montebello, one of the large mansions along this road, the rear of which was visible from the path earlier. Opposite its gate lodge, turn left into Horseshoe Lane, following the red and yellow arrows. This is a private unmade road, lined by opulent looking houses, eventually becoming a track. At the end of this cross a stile into the field, and follow the path straight on, signposted Mays Lane. This section can be muddy. Enter the next field, following the line of power cables. High Barnet is visible ahead to the right. After the open fields, the path becomes a grassy track between hedges.

Cross the stile and follow the arrows and power lines straight ahead across the middle of the next field. Go through a kissing gate marked with a traffic light set of red, yellow and green arrows, and then cross Dollis Brook via the metal bridge. A piggery next to the bridge explains the odours. Turn right to follow the banks of the brook and you will now follow the green arrows for a while. These mark the route of the recently-established Dollis Valley Greenwalk, a 14-mile route from Moat Mount all the way to Hampstead Heath, using open space along the route of Dollis Brook and Mutton Brook. The brooks act as extremely valuable wildlife corridors into the urban space.

Follow the Greenwalk past playing fields, across a fenced track, and into the next meadow. Beyond this, the walk goes through mown grassland and you should follow the tarmac path a little to the left of the brook. Ignore a yellow arrow indicating a footbridge to the fields opposite, then a little later take the right fork, following the Greenwalk.

Cross Barnet Lane, turn right and then left, following the arrows at Mapboard No. 2, which carries information about the Greenwalk, and explaining how the council tries to keep grassland next to Dollis Brook. Follow the track between the buildings, go through the car park, then take the tarmac path at the edge of the playing fields. There is open grassland and playing fields on the other side of the brook. At the end of the recreational area, turn right to exit via the corner by the electricity substation. Stay on the tarmac path following the brook. Cross – but do not take – the cyclepath, keeping to the tarmac footpath. The houses approach closely to the brook here. The path now goes through Brook Farm Open Space, formerly a working farm. This is now parkland with trees and shrubs, with some new tree planting. The area to the left is bounded by the Northern line, and you eventually come to Totteridge Lane, by Totteridge and Whetstone station.

Cross the road, turning to right and then left following the arrows, and continue on the tarmac path. Ignore a smaller fork to the right, staying on the main path. Shortly after this, follow the red and green arrows across the bridge over the brook.

You leave the marked Greenwalk here, so ignore further signs and turn right up Laurel Way. Go to the end, passing the bollards, and, turning right onto the path, duck under the chest-high barrier and enter the very pretty Totteridge Village area. There is a duck pond on the left, and broad verges either side of the road. Pass the cricket club, and come to the village green, fringed by trees. Walk by the left of the green, and pass the school, part of which was Kemp Hall, previously owned by Lord Kemp of Kemp's Biscuits. Turn left at Totteridge Village (the road) and pass the front of the school to return to the pub.

# Shepperton
## The King's Head

The King's Head is a 14th century inn, idyllically placed in the village square next to the church. The pub has a number of small bars and nooks and crannies connected by narrow passageways with flagstones underfoot and beams overhead. A pub of this age accumulates stories, such as that Nell Gwynne stayed here (possibly with Charles II) and more recently, Richard Burton and Elizabeth Taylor are said to have staged a sausage roll fight here (presumably relaxing after filming). Charles Dickens mentioned the pub in *Oliver Twist.*

A Courage house, the pub has Courage Best, Wadworth 6X and a guest beer on handpump, Dry Blackthorn Cider on draught, and a range of bottled lagers and wines.

Excellent hot and cold food, from sandwiches to three-course meals, is available Monday to Saturday. Main courses include steak, scampi, plaice, calamari and quiche, with the house specialities being Shepperton Pie (a shepherd's pie with cheese on top and 'secret ingredients') and special home-made Welsh rarebit. Jacket potatoes, salads and sandwiches are also available, as is a choice of desserts such as treacle tart and apple pie.

There is a small patio at the rear, some of which is under cover.

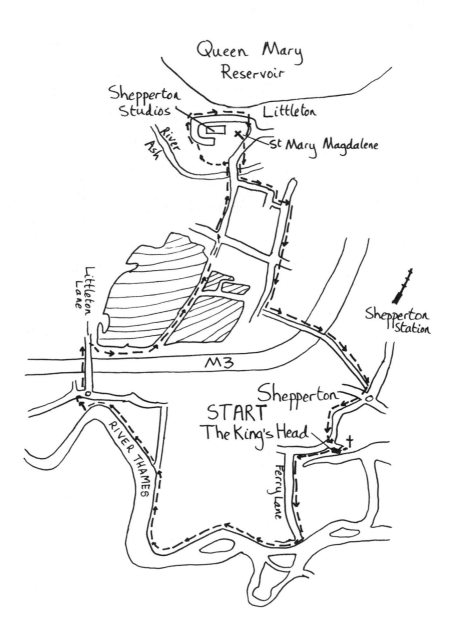

Queen Mary
Reservoir

Shepperton
Studios

Littleton

River
Ash

St Mary Magdalene

Littleton
Lane

Shepperton
Station

M3

Shepperton

START
The King's Head

RIVER THAMES

Ferry Lane

Children can eat with their parents, especially on the patio.

Opening hours are Monday-Friday 11 am-3 pm, 5.30 pm-11 pm; Saturday 11 am-11 pm; Sunday 12 noon-3 pm, 7 am-10.30 pm. Food served Monday-Saturday 12 noon-2 pm, 7.30 pm-10 pm (no food on Sundays). Telephone: 0932 221910.

*How to get there:* The inn is in Church Road, Shepperton. Russell Road (B375) leads through Shepperton and Church Road branches off at the roundabout, towards the river. The pub is on Church Square. Nearest railway station: Shepperton (Waterloo line).

*Parking:* There may be some space in the village square (often full), and a public car park is close by at Manor Park.

*Length of the walk:* 5½ miles (inn GR 077666).

*This walk takes you past much open water, The Thames and gravel-pit lakes (with many opportunities to see waterfowl), as well as the picturesque old village of Shepperton, Littleton Church and round the perimeter of Shepperton Studios.*

## The Walk

Leave the pub and explore Shepperton church. Leave the church via the front gates, walk through the village square and turn left onto Church Road/Chertsey Road. Pass Creek House on the left and Church House on the right. Next to this, Little Cottage is designated a building of Special Interest by Surrey County Council. Turn left onto Ferry Lane, signposted 'Pedestrian Ferry'; take care, there is no footpath.

At the river, turn right to follow the towpath (a road at this point). Keep straight on past the lock and Lock Island, then use the footpath at the river's edge to pass the weir and Pharaoh's Island. From here on you get a fine view of the river, the select housing on either side (most with private moorings) and the associated boats. A range of waterfowl can also be seen. When the road veers to the right, take the public footpath signposted straight ahead.

You are now on a broad grass path with willows and other trees bordering the river and a hedge to the right. The houses on the right become fewer and older and the scene to the left becomes more rural. After a fairly straight stretch of river, go through a metal kissing gate and turn right to leave this open field via a stile in the corner onto Chertsey Bridge Road.

Turn right for the roundabout, and turn left there onto Littleton Lane. Cross over the M3, and at the end of the bridge turn right onto a footpath leading downhill. At the bottom, follow a track between the M3 and the wire fence of a yachting club. Ignore an almost overgrown path to the left by an old gatepost and keep parallel to the M3 until a little way further on a more clearly-defined path leads to the left over a small plank bridge out towards a narrow strip of land between two lakes. Keep the wire fence on your left, and cross over a bridge spanning a connection between the lakes. The lake on the right comes to an end, and wilderness gives way to houses on the right.

Keep following the shore of the lake on the left and come out onto Fairview Drive. Keep straight on and across the crossroads with Laleham Road into Squires Bridge Road. Cross the river Ash at Squires Bridge – look to your left to see the figure (of a reclining Neptune?) in the middle of the river. Immediately after crossing the bridge, turn left through a gateway into parkland bordering the river.

Follow the path bordering the river and the studio perimeter until the studios end and the housing estate starts. Take the first exit to the right and emerge into Wilcox Gardens and then onto Studios Road. Go straight ahead towards the embankment of the Queen Mary reservoir, built in 1925, one of the largest in the world, capable (when full) of supplying London for one month. Follow the road round to the right, passing studios, pieces of discarded scenery and the main entrance. Some classic films were made at Shepperton Studios for British Lion films, including the non-location filming for *The Third Man* and *The African Queen*. At the end of the studio complex, come out onto Squires Bridge Road, turn right and walk to the church.

The church of St. Mary Magdalene was founded in the 12th century, by monks from nearby Chertsey Abbey, but most of the building is 13th century. Leave the church, and turn right to return to the bridge over the river Ash. After crossing this, turn left into Ash Road, right at Wood Road, then almost immediately after, turn left into Petts Lane. Turn right onto Watersplash Road. Pass the Barley Mow pub, then go straight across the crossroads with Laleham Road, passing The Bull, to go down Sheep Walk. Pass the end of Mandeville Road on the right, and the derelict site of a former school, then turn left onto a public footpath leading through a wilderness area flanked by trees. Cross the M3 by the footbridge, then continue on the path, following the line of the stream, which contributes to a good wildlife habitat. The footpath becomes School Lane. Follow this past The Three Horseshoes and turn right at the main road.

Go across the roundabout with the war memorial at the centre to enter Church Road. Shepperton Manor Park, and a public car park, are on the left. Pass Manor House Court on the left and some attractive groups of 16th century cottages. At the village square, look to the left, keeping the garage behind you, for the best view of the square with its fine row of 18th century cottages. Return to the King's Head.

# 29 Ickenham
## The Coach and Horses

Ickenham has preserved the traditional central village grouping of pond, pump, pub and parish church. The Coach and Horses forms part of this group, behind the village pump. Parts of the pub are said to be over 400 years old, and, as a major public building at the village centre, it acted as courthouse. The pub is full of nooks and crannies, especially in the older part, and some original beams can still be seen. Children and dogs are asked to stay in the large garden which is surrounded by trees and has a play area at one end.

The beers served in this Taylor Walker house are Benskins Bitter, Ind Coope, Burton and Tetley Bitter with guest ales. Löwenbrau Lager and Old English Cider are on draught. 'K' and Norfolk Classic bottled ciders are available. Opening times are Monday to Thursday 11 am to 3.30 pm, 5.30 pm to 11 pm; Fridays and Saturdays 11 am to 11 pm, Sunday hours are standard.

Food is served from 12 noon-2.30 pm, and in the evenings (not Sundays) 'if not busy', usually until 8 pm. From Monday to Friday there is a full menu, covering sandwiches, salads, jacket potatoes and four daily hot specials, and on Sundays a roast lunch is featured. On Saturdays, only sandwiches and jacket potatoes are served. On some summer Saturdays there is a barbecue – on these days hot food is available after 2.30 pm. Telephone: 0895 632184.

*How to get there:* The pub is at the junction of Long Lane (B466) and Swakeleys Road (B467). Nearest station: Ickenham (Metropolitan and Piccadilly lines – Piccadilly peak hours only).

*Parking:* In the pub car park.

*Length of the walk:* 6¾ miles (inn GR 080862).

*Starting in the centre of Ickenham, the walk begins with a miniature railway, if you come at the right time. You pass Ickenham church and shortly after you see the exterior of Swakeleys, a fine 17th century mansion. The walk follows the river Pinn out of Ickenham, then goes across country (you may encounter some mud), and a golf course, to reach some lakes and the Grand Union Canal. The towpath leads you into Uxbridge, and you return to Ickenham via Uxbridge Common and a wood.*

## The Walk

If this is the first Saturday of the month, the Ickenham Miniature Railway will be open. Turn right leaving the pub and follow the path down to its track. It runs from 12 noon-5.30 pm or dusk from the first Saturday in April until December.

Return to the pump, cross the road and enter St. Giles's churchyard. The church dates from the 14th century, the brick north aisle having been added in the 16th century. Leaving the church, turn right along Swakeleys Road, cross over, and turn left along The Avenue, a quiet private road with secluded houses on both sides initially, then woodland on the right. Opposite the end of Milton Road, turn right onto a tarmac path going through the parkland. Follow this to the left and arrive at a small lake. Just to the left of the end of this, go through a small gate leading to a path following the left side of the lake. The trees soon thin out on the left to give you a view of Swakeleys, a redbrick mansion built 1630-1638 by Sir Edward Wright, Lord Mayor of London 1640-41.

Follow the path round the edge of the grounds, leave via the drive and gate, and turn right onto Swakeleys Lane. Pass the end of the lake, then turn right into the parkland. Walk along the left hand edge of the parkland, following the river Pinn. Pass to the left of a play area, ignore a metal footbridge, and follow the path by the hedge and then by the tennis courts to re-emerge into woodland. Take the path to the left following the Pinn, then stay on the main path as the Pinn veers away to the left. The path comes out onto Swakeleys Road. Turn left, cross the road, continue over the bridge, then turn right into the

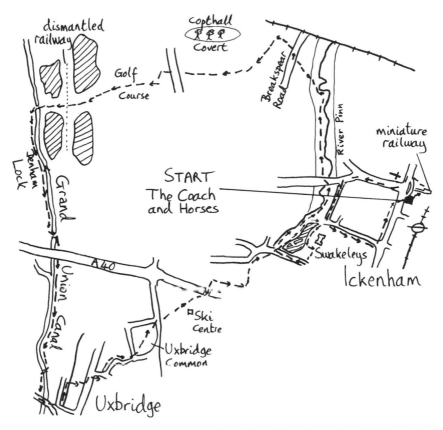

parkland with the river on your right. Trees line the edge of the park, and wild flowers and shrubs grow along the riverbank, making a haven for insects and birds. Keep straight on past a footbridge, remaining on the left of the Pinn. Follow the main path through a wood of small trees along the river, skirting the edge of a dry(ish) moat. Cross into the neighbouring field via the stile.

Follow the edge of the field to the first line of trees, then strike out across the field to the stile at the foot of the large oak (by the footpath sign). Climb over the stile into Breakspear Road (careful, no footpath), turn right, then within 20 yards, turn left at the footpath signpost, and walk down the track, following a yellow Colne Valley Park footpath arrow (this is the right way, not a private drive). Turn left at the fence, and cross the stile into the field, following the yellow arrows. Keep to the edge of the field, and cross the stile at the end.

Keep to the right hand edge of the next field. You are now in open countryside. Go across two fields, aiming for stiles in the centre of the hedges, passing the wooded Copthall Covert, and reaching the road via another stile. Cross Harvil Road and the stile opposite, then cross this field, aiming for a stile to the half left. Cross this stile and follow the yellow arrow across the next field and stile to emerge on the municipal golf course. Follow the public footpath across this, taking due care. The footpath turns off the gravel drive after a couple of holes to run across a grassy practice green – keep an eye on the signposts. Leave the golf course, following the yellow arrow. There are now lakes on both sides of the path, attracting plenty of waterfowl. Cross the track of a dismantled railway, enter the wood, cross the plank bridge and walk between two more lakes, and then reach the Grand Union Canal. Cross the bridge over it and turn left to follow the towpath on the right of the canal.

At Denham Lock, refreshments can be had at the lock keeper's cottage – Fran's Tea Gardens. Just beyond the lock, the river Colne flows next to the canal. Follow the towpath all the way into Uxbridge, passing some meadows and crossing and then recrossing the canal via the bridges. At Uxbridge Lock leave the canal at the bridge and turn left. Pass the Crown and Treaty pub on the right, the site of unsuccessful peace talks between the Royalists and Parliamentarians in the Civil War, and converted into a pub about 1802. Follow the old line of the High Street straight on, and turn left at the footpath sign into Braybourne Close. Turn off the pavement and follow the footpath by Fray's River on the right. Cross the river at the footbridge and follow the path uphill, crossing the road and continue to Harefield Road. Turn left, then right into Fairfield Road, left into Cornwall Road, following this round to the right, and turn left at the T junction to come to Uxbridge Common.

Cross the common diagonally to meet the main road at the far corner, then cross the dual carriageway and go through the gate, following the public footpath sign. The gravel path becomes a track to the left of the ski centre and to the right of playing fields. Leave the track and walk round the edge of the playing field to come to the left of a hedge, and head for the trees at the end. Turn right onto a tarmac path at the edge of the field marked by a row of lamp posts, and follow the path through the woods, and then over the A40 by the footbridge (Vyners Bridge). Turn right and follow the fence round Vyners school playing field, turning left at the end, right at Warren Road, then right onto Swakeleys Lane. Turn left into the Swakeleys parkland, and this time follow the tarmac path on the right by the lake, with its two islands and ducks. Follow the lake to the parkland exit, and continue straight down Milton Road. Turn left at Long Lane, and walk along this to the pub.

# Harefield
## The White Horse

The White Horse, in Church Hill, is of 16th century origin, used first as cottages, then as an inn from 1625. In 1779 it was owned by Stephen Salter, brewer of Richmond. The Salter Brewery merged with Ind Coope, and it is now a Greenalls house. Like many rural pubs, it was occasionally used for official purposes. An inquest was held here in 1889, and, it is said, a murderer was once held overnight in the cellar (for a fee to the publican).

The interior now is in fact very cosy and comfortable, with a split-level saloon bar, the upper level being arranged for dining, where children may eat with their parents. The public bar has recently been converted into a carpeted village bar with an open fire. There is a large family garden outside. The pub has a large lovable Newfoundland dog ('Ruddles'), but as he gets territorially minded if other dogs are brought in, please keep your dog outside.

A good range of hot and cold home-cooked food is served seven days a week, ranging from standard fare such as sandwiches, ploughman's lunches, pizzas and burgers, to imaginative and tempting house specialities such as Louisiana catfish and Caribbean chicken. A range of starters and hot puddings and prestige ice creams are available, so that you can enjoy a three-course meal here. Food is available at lunchtimes 12 noon-2.15 pm (2.30 pm on Sundays) and in the evenings Monday-Saturday 6.30 pm-10 pm and Sundays 7 pm-9.45 pm. Barbecues are held in the garden in summer.

Beers served are Wadsworth 6X, Tetley Yorkshire Bitter, Abbot (guest beer), Greenalls Original, Bitter and Dark Mild; additional guest beers may be carried. Addlestone's cask conditioned cider is on draught.

Opening times are Monday-Saturday 12 noon-3 pm and 6 pm-11 pm, Sunday 12 noon-3 pm and 7 pm-10.30 pm.

Telephone: 0895 822144.

*How to get there:* The inn is on Church Hill, Harefield. Harvil Road leads north from the B467 just outside Ickenham, becoming Church Hill near Harefield church. The pub is on the left shortly after the church, before the centre of Harefield. Nearest stations: Northwood (Metropolitan line), Uxbridge (Piccadilly – peak hours only – and Metropolitan lines), and you can walk to Newyears Green from West Ruislip (Central line). Denham (BR) – walk along Moorfield Road then Moorhall Road which crosses the canal, then either continue with the walk by turning right at Dellside, or go straight to the pub by turning left at Harvil Road. Bus 347/348 runs past the pub at least hourly to Uxbridge one way and Northwood the other.

*Parking:* Restricted pub car park.

*Length of the walk:* 5½ miles (inn GR 051898).

*This is the most rural of the walks in this book, and has everything. You will recognise all of our favourite features of a good walk: waterways, woods, a quiet cemetery and a picturesque church. The walk passes through some very attractive rolling countryside, and there are many opportunities to see wildlife and wonderful views and get muddy boots. There are stiles to climb and some gentle slopes.*

**The Walk**
Leave the pub, turn left and continue up the hill. Just before the layby for the bus stop, turn left onto the public footpath. Cross one road and continue down the footpath opposite. This soon leaves the houses and becomes rural. Cross a stile and keep straight on following the sign to Black Jack Lock. On your left after a little way is a good view of the Colne valley, lakes and waterways. Climb a stile at the end of the path, and turn left down a track following the signpost. This descends following the edge of the field, coming to another stile. The Grand Union Canal is visible below. Turn right and follow the sign diagonally across the field to leave it by a stile near the canal. Follow

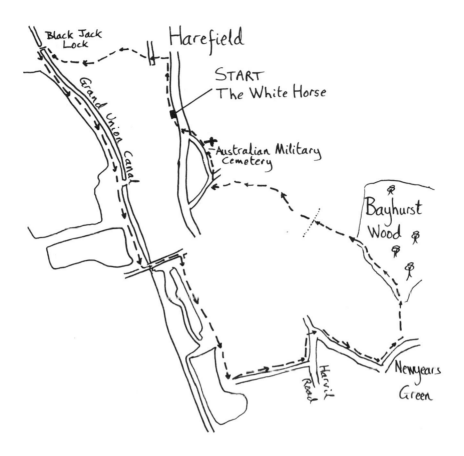

the lane ahead, then turn left and cross the canal via the bridge. Go
to the lock, then come back under the bridge on the towpath.

The path is surrounded by water, the canal on the left and the lake
on the right, used as a marina, acting as a haven for a great number
of waterfowl. Near a disused bridge, the water on the right is
shallower, attracting waders; after the bridge, the canal broadens, and
the far bank attracts reed-dwelling birds. The large gravel extraction
plant on the right explains the origin of the large lakes.

Leave the canal at a lock and road bridge by going up the steps to
the right of the towpath. Turn left onto Moorhall Road, crossing the
canal, then pass an office development on the left, turn right at
Dellside, and follow a signposted footpath. Cross the stile at the end
of the path, and keep straight on at the edge of the field. Pass the end
of a small copse separating two fields, keep straight on, and walk

under power lines. At the start of a planted field there is a signpost and stile. Cross the stile and follow the right hand side of the hedge in the next mowed field. Leave this on to the road. Do not follow the footpath sign, but turn left and follow the lane past the brick ivy-covered farmhouse. At the main road (Harvil Road), turn left and then take the first turn right, enticingly signposted 'Household Waste Site'.

This is Newyears Green Lane. Follow it past Newyears Farm and a pond, and then just after where the power cables cross the road, turn left onto the footpath indicated by the yellow arrow, crossing the stile, and keeping to the left of the wooden fence – there is a bridleway on the right. Follow the path towards Bayhurst Wood. Cross one stile, continuing at the field edge, and then another, continuing on the bridleway for a few yards, and then enter the wood, under the single bar fence to exclude horses. Now inside the wood, follow the path parallel to the fence. Keep straight on at the end of the field on the left and the path is crossed by a path from the field. Ignore a broader bridlepath running parallel on the right, pass to the right of the pond, ignore a path leading uphill, staying on a path winding through the trees and to the left of the bridlepath. At the point where the path is crossed by a path leading uphill (with the sign 'no horses') turn left to cross the stile and leave the wood.

Keep to the side of the field and go under the power lines. There is a superb view of rolling countryside here, and of Breakspear House to the right. Cross the stile at the end of the field, and then the path to climb the stile opposite, following the red markings. Keep straight on, cross a stile with red markings at the edge of the field, keep to the edge of the field, and cross a stile with green markings at the end. Keep straight on through the small wood, cross a stile and follow the footpath across the next field to the right of the hedge.

Veer right at the bottom, following the hedge and footpath sign. Cross a stile into the next field, and then at the end, cross a stile to the left (yellow arrow). Cross another stile at the end, then strike out half right across the next field to a stile at the foot of the tree. You are passing a ruined walled garden, the remnants of Harefield Place, demolished in 1814.

Cross the stile, turn right onto the gravel track, then turn left. On the right is the Australian military cemetery, for troops who died at Harefield Hospital in the Second World War.

Next to this is St. Mary's church, described by Pevsner as 'an irregular picturesque little building'. It is mainly 14th century, with some 13th century work, and many later alterations. The church may be small, but it is packed with monuments. Leave the church, turning right and right again at the main road. Pass almshouses on the right, founded by Alice, Countess of Derby. Continue along to the pub.